from
KITCHEN
to
CAREER

by Adele Lewis and Edith Bobroff
FROM COLLEGE TO CAREER
FROM KITCHEN TO CAREER

from
KITCHEN
to
CAREER

by Adele Lewis and Edith Bobroff

THE BOBBS-MERRILL COMPANY, INC.
A Subsidiary of Howard W. Sams & Co., Inc.
Publishers • INDIANAPOLIS • KANSAS CITY • NEW YORK

First printing, 1965
Copyright © 1965 by Adele Lewis and Edith Bobroff
All rights reserved
Library of Congress Catalog card number 64-66343

Printed in the United States of America

to
William M. Lewis
and
Jason Marks

CONTENTS

Preface		ix
Introduction		xi
I	The Orientation	3
II	Tinker, Tailor ...	12
III	You	18
IV	Testing	37
V	Back to School	45
VI	Never Too Late for a Profession	69
VII	Office Life	93
VIII	Develop a Technical Skill	113
IX	A Business of Your Own	144
X	Spare Time Dollars	156
XI	Careers with the Government	163
A Final Word		191
Index		195

PREFACE

This, our second book about careers, would seem a natural successor to our first, called *From College to Career*. It is, in fact, not a sequel, but almost a parallel. We have found from our some fifteen years as employment counselors that the "returnee" to the labor market, as well as the mature woman who has never worked, faces her situation with the same perplexity, and in some cases, dismay, as the college graduate. We have even found in some instances that there is greater naïveté on the part of the mature woman than the college grad. Many women who want to go to work either have had little or no job experience, or worked perhaps ten or fifteen years before in a clerical job prior to getting married.

Every year, hundreds of mature women stop into Career Blazers seeking advice. Before setting foot into what is for them a great unknown, they want to know what to do, whether there will be a market for them, what they can expect, what fields are open to them, will they have to go back to school—in essence, "Where do we go from here?"

Our efforts to give these women the best guidance possible impelled us to conduct our own research into this as yet hardly explored subject of jobs for the older woman. We learned, to our amazement, that although there was a President's Commission to study the needs and opportunities for women returning to work, sev-

FROM KITCHEN TO CAREER

eral schools and colleges developing special courses of study, and one or two organizations attempting to assess and help the woman to make her big step, there is *no* place where a woman can go to get a comprehensive picture of what to expect.

In a modest way, we have in *From Kitchen to Career* attempted to synthesize the various efforts now being made. This book represents only a beginning. Even now as you read it, more and more opportunities are opening up, both in accelerated educational programs and in available work. Essentially, this book will serve as an initial guide. You don't jump off the diving board until you know how to swim, and from this book, you should be able to master some of the vital strokes.

Another important area covered by this book is the possibility of a career at age thirty, forty, even fifty and sixty. Given the drive, energy, ambition—and the right direction—there simply is no telling what a woman will be able to do.

We wish to thank those many applicants whose probing and thoughtful questions led to our research. They, it might be said, "unknowingly" wrote the book. We also wish to thank the many personnel directors who were never too busy to answer our queries, as well as the numerous educators and members of professional organizations who not only replied to our questionnaire surveys, but also equipped us with invaluable source material.

Finally, we are especially indebted to our splendid office staff for their moral support, to Dr. Isidore Portnoy for his inspiring counsel, and to Jason Marks for his outstanding technical assistance.

INTRODUCTION

Maturity in years means many things. It may mean the ability to handle one's responsibilities. Or it may mean being able to look forward to retirement as the children grow up, marry and produce their own families. It may also signal the end of a long, hard financial pull. For the mature woman—the woman in her forties—the years that lie ahead hold forth the promise of a new life. Far from being old, or worn out, or decrepit, the woman in her forties whose family responsibilities are decreasing is nowadays vitally concerned with making effective use of her time, rather than hiding her light under a bushel of social engagements, clubs, and teas. Usefulness, constructiveness, productivity—bywords that in the past have inspired youthful energies—today strike a profoundly sympathetic chord in the mind and heart of the "over 40" gal. Our society has aided and abetted this gentle revolutionary spirit among women. Whatever her age, the female is constantly urged to "stay young, feel young, live young." The end result of this "youth campaign" is to keep the mature woman on her toes. She begins to appreciate her own worth and to realize that she is an alert, dynamic individual at the top of her powers. She will not take a back seat to anyone—and why should she when she belongs in the driver's seat?

Granted that she has the energy, the ability, and the motivation, how does the woman of forty express her new-found freedom? Mainly, she becomes a job seeker. It is only natural that after having immolated herself on the altar of kitchen-kinder routine for some fifteen or twenty years, the mature woman should be enticed by the prospect of being able to win her place in the "fascinating outside world." If she has never worked in an office she may fall easy prey to the fantasy that holding down an office position is one gay whirl of meeting VIPs, attending banquets and dinner parties, and sharing in important policy-making decisions. If she aspires to do something "professionally," she may be tempted by the individual "freedom" a profession has to offer—letting dreams of glory blind her to the reality that a great deal of work and education are necessary to the making of a professional. Almost invariably, our "over 40" charmer gift-wraps her vague, albeit laudable ambition of going back to work with the gaudy verbal deception, "If I present myself, there will be a job for me."

Little does she know! And little did *we* know until we started researching this book and exploring that largely undiscovered domain graced by the woman over 40—her aspirations, her tremendous potential, the jobs now available to her, and the possibilities of realizing her abilities in the business world. What started us thinking and digging and investigating was an incident that happened recently at Career Blazers. We interviewed a woman in her early forties who was looking for a job. This attractive mother of two had married right after graduating from college and settled down to raise babies. As a result, she never had the opportunity

INTRODUCTION

to hold a job. When she came to us, her older child had just entered college and the younger was in her junior year of high school. Our applicant radiated personality and probably possessed a great deal of latent ability, but when she offered herself with a "Here I am, now it's your turn," we were stymied. Certainly, we were able to make a few standard suggestions: Learn some stenographic and typing skills or the fundamentals of bookkeeping, get some training on a telephone-answering board, or possibly return to school and study to become a teacher, social worker, etc. Unfortunately, we were in the same position as most other private and public agencies—much as they would like to help this type of job seeker, they are simply unable to divert precious hours from other urgent matters to determine where her capabilities and interests might lie, and thereby give her the direction she needs and deserves.

The back-to-work woman is somewhat of a phenomenon in our society. Because she remains an innovation, the number of sources to which she can refer for guidance is minimal indeed. There are, of course, some organizations designed to aid her, such as the Seven College Vocational Workshops, Barnard College, 606 West 120 Street, New York 10027; but generally speaking, all of us—the woman herself, the counselor, and the prospective employer—are in the same boat. We are all at sea! Ordinarily we chirp suitable sympathy and admiration and tell ourselves, "These women are a great untapped force in the job world" and let it go at that, like Uncle Amos with a "Now, could be . . ."

Could be? We prefer—WILL BE! At Career Blazers, we have watched with excitement this mounting trend by women over 40 toward collecting paychecks instead of green stamps. And because so many mature women have told us that they want to go back to work, we have undertaken this study of the job market as it applies to their needs. The findings have been most gratifying. We have learned that not only are there many jobs to be had, but that with the proper preparation, a woman who has reached forty can still have a career. Choosing her field with reason and care, she can, without further waste of time, retrain herself in an area that will put to use her precious years of life experience. She can plan the next thirty years of her life so that her interests, productivity and potential will continue to grow.

Fountain of Youth? We can't claim to have discovered it. But we do put the question: In what better way can a woman retain her youthfulness of spirit and appearance than by staying interested in, and excited by, the work she is doing? Self-growth is the cure for the "I'm a fifth wheel" blues, that depressive state we sink into when we're feeling useless and unproductive. Of course, planning ahead is essential to personal progress. We have to know what our goals are, and our best means of attaining them. Healthy, happy people are those who are guided by a firm sense of direction and involved in a fulfilling experience.

An especially encouraging development in America today is the way schools, industry, and government are all pitching in to help the woman who wants to return to work. There is a general realization that the mature woman has a world of ability to offer the prospective employer. Educators, for example, have been hammering away at the theme that a well-trained woman can handle a job every bit as competently as a man. The

INTRODUCTION

late President Kennedy appointed women to high governmental office and now President Johnson has stepped up the procedure. The latter, in particular, has made it quite clear that he intends to utilize woman-power to its fullest.

Some startling facts about the working woman have been furnished by the U. S. Department of Labor's Bureau of Statistics. In 1920, the average age of the working girls was 28; today, it is about 40! It would appear from these figures that nowadays:

1. A woman spends the early years of her marriage raising a family;
2. is ready to go back to work when her children have reached school age; and
3. expects to work for a considerable period of time.

The Bureau of Statistics also announced that the biggest jump in female employment has taken place among those in the 45-to-54 year-old age bracket! Furthermore, in the years from 1951 to 1961 inclusive, the number of married women in the work force climbed to a high of 4.2 million.

These statistics, taken at their face value, appear to indicate that not only are women returning to the job market in increasing numbers, but also that they aren't leaving their jobs. What's behind this mass movement? Of all the inducements that beckon the mature woman back to employment, the idea of leading a useful and productive life seems to be the strongest.

We are fortunate to live in a country where there is freedom of choice. Within the limits of our capacity we can choose our own line of work or course of study. We can also think, vote, and worship as we please. Interestingly enough, today's mature woman may be one of the freest individuals in our society. The opportunities are such that she no longer need feel useless once she has sent her children out into the world. She is able to go back to work, and her choice of job may range from one that involves a name and title on the door to part-time, fill-in "fun" employment. With a little extra effort, she may get that second chance that many men in her age group yearn for, but can never achieve. Many adults (especially men supporting families) find out all too late that the job choice they made at twenty is not what they really want to do at forty!

Given the opportunity, the back-to-work woman can make the next twenty or thirty years of her life a period of rewarding activity and self-fulfillment. In this book, the authors attempt to outline a number of paths that she may follow to reach her goal, suggest some short-cuts to success, and cite pitfalls to be avoided. We have not been able to cover every job or educational opportunity—this book should serve mainly as an introduction to what is available. The rest, as in every area of life, is up to you.

PART ONE

CHAPTER I | *The Orientation*

Hunting for a job can be either a catastrophe or an exhilarating experience. It can set you back twenty psychological years or it can pyramid you to the pinnacle of self-confidence. From our long experience at Career Blazers we have come to the conclusion that there is an art to the hunting-for, and the getting-of, a job. It is an art that is easily learned, but too often disregarded or discarded. Like any other art, it requires some training and definitely some thoughtful analysis before it can be performed successfully. We intend to reveal this art to you, step by step. In some cases, the process of acquiring it may seem mundane (especially when we mention such words as stenography and typing). In other instances, the prospect of going back to school may loom as a cumbersome and expensive proposition. But we guarantee that what at first appears to be the long way around often turns out to be the shortest route. Bear with us while we outline various plans of action.

How do you define a "winner"? The winner is simply a person who gets whatever he or she goes after—

whether it be a job, a sale, admission to college, or any number of other important achievements. From where we sit, the winner is the applicant who gets the job. Why is it that some people are offered every position for which they're interviewed, while others are continually rejected? We have found that getting the job has nothing to do with how old you are, what faith you observe, what the color of your skin happens to be, or whether you're a man or a woman. We have been able to place proportionately the same number of mature women as we have younger people. When a trainee cannot get a job, she usually blames her failure on her lack of experience. "All the companies say I'm too young, too inexperienced," she complains. When a more mature person cannot secure a job, she reverses the argument with the assertion, "All the companies say I'm over-qualified." Often a Negro woman failing to win a position will attach the entire blame to her color. And then there is the consummate rationalization for the woman over forty—her indulgence in the mistaken belief that organizations will never hire an older woman and that she is being discriminated against because of her age.

Fortunately, our experience has proved that a woman's age is not the determining factor in why jobs are won or lost. At either extreme the complaints have only a limited validity. For while the youngster is lamenting that her green years have hamstrung her job-hunting effort, the self-same company that interviewed her may be busy hiring a young lady *exactly* her age! And the same employer whom our more mature woman berated for a "lack of sympathy" may that very moment have been considering the promotion of a number of competent female employees! Young and old, Negro and white, Christian and Jew— in every group we find those who believe they failed because "they're the unlucky ones." There are the mature in years who say that the young get all the breaks, and the young who insist that the ripe plums off the employment tree always seem to fall into the lap of the older person. There are the college graduates who claim that no one respects a college degree; and the high school grads who say that their four years of study add up to a mere pig in a poke for the prospective employer, who will hire you only if you have a college degree.

Group, or individual, self-pity never won anyone a blue ribbon, nor a coveted job. Success, we have observed, lies in the proper use of knowledge, foresight, and action.

Know Yourself, Your Market and What To Aim for

Have a thorough awareness of your assets as well as your limitations. Then balance these against the opportunities and limitations that prevail in the job market. At Career Blazers we have found that generally there is no discrimination because of age, nor is there any general prejudice against the older woman, even if she has no working experience. Some types of jobs do, in fact, call for an older woman's poise and maturity. However, there are also fields of endeavor which by their very nature stalemate the older woman's efforts to break into them. Certain glamour vineyards, for example, frown on any member of the staff who is not perky, even perhaps a little sexy. Other jobs such as editor, copywriter, etc.—require a quite specific training which the hausfrau newly unshackled from the stove is not likely to possess. We have been intrigued to find that many of the fantasies held by the trainee, high school or college graduate are also shared by the older woman returning to work. The English major who pursues job offers for editors at $150 a week or for copywriters at $250 a week on the strength of having written for her college yearbook, is doomed to the same disappointment as the mature woman avid for these same positions, who wrote sparkling copy to promote her hometown PTA's annual dinner dance-and-social. Persistence in an ill-advised search for that-which-is-unachievable-without-more-training-and-experience (a search which can seem as long as the previous hyphenated mouthful!) can only lead to an intense discouragement that gradually dissolves into rage and hostility. As the feeling of "Nobody wants me" deepens, the job seeker finds that she is becoming emotionally crippled.

Be Realistic

An honest appraisal of your talents, your skills, and your ability, plus a plan to improve yourself in certain rusty areas are your keys to success. Be realistic about the job market. If you want to be a television receptionist or a World's Fair hostess, chances are you are headed toward the proverbial brick wall. The zany glamour fields are usually staffed by young men and women with enough energy to launch an Atlas missile. There is a logical reason for this. The young people seem to have the stamina to sustain the lively, almost frenetic pace which the communication arts demand of their toiling members. The young have the flexibility to work at all hours, even far into the night. In many instances, they are not tied down by family responsibilities requiring a routine schedule. And let's face it, these are the fields that are constantly touting the beautiful face and figure. It's awfully difficult to look at forty the way you did at twenty. Few of us can, or want to, compete on this level! The mature worker really does have more to offer than her looks and figure.

Most of the trainee jobs that are advertised are definitely not for the older worker. In the majority of these ads, the word "trainee" implies a person who is suited to handling a myriad of chores, many of them quite menial. The trainee's job in many cases is larded with such duties as running down for coffee, going to the post office, or doing the boss's personal shopping. While you are in every sense a trainee yourself, what you specifically want is to learn a particular field. It is a hard thing for an employer to ask a mature person, especially one who is older than himself, to run an errand. Nor would the average mature woman want such a job—although the title that goes with it might hold some allure. It is also wise to steer clear of careers where there is a notable shortage of jobs. You might have a voice that would turn a nightingale green with envy, yet pursuing a career in radio-announcing, for example, is not likely to be a good choice. To succeed in photography, you must be better than average. To establish yourself as a writer—you must be superlative (except perhaps in the realm of government, where the competition is not as keen).

Nobody Wants Me ...

Not so. Maturity and dignity count for a great deal in this world. From the untrained receptionist who graciously greets famous people to the appointee on the Atomic Energy Commission (Mrs. Mary Bunting, 1964), industry and government are desperately looking for the right woman to fit their growing needs. At this writing, women are reportedly employed in close to 450 individual occupations, including such unlikely endeavors as those of electrician, carpenter, and paperhanger! The field is as vast as the mature woman's aspiration to succeed, and range from scientist, physicist, mathematician, teacher (all levels), social worker, physical therapist, occupational therapist, executive, administrative assistant, secretary, bookkeeper to clerical worker, hostess, and taxi driver. For a complete list of the jobs we have covered, turn to the Job Glossary Index at the back of the book.

Whatever area of work you finally decide upon, your commitment to follow through will be your passport to success. Experts agree that the woman who brings her skills up to date with today's developments will become of far greater value in the job world than the one who has been on the job for years but has not kept in step with progress.

Plan of Action

Looking for a job is far easier than looking for a needle in the proverbial haystack. Often the choice of job will in itself direct the proper approach to use. The standard sources are personal friends and relatives, newspaper advertisements, public and private employment agencies, college placement offices and your own direct mail campaign.

Let's Be Personal

Don't let pride stand in your way. Many women tell

us that they prefer not to use the influence of friends or relatives in getting jobs. They want to do it alone. This attitude is one that elicits admiration, but may not get the job. If you do know of a person who can speak for you, then by all means use your contact. You will not be hired if you do not qualify, but employers are human also. If they hear from a source which they respect that such and such a person is an especially fine candidate, they are more than likely to favor this candidate. An employer invests time and money every time he hires a new person. He wants to be sure that he has made the best possible choice.

Newspaper Advertisements

When you begin your job hunt, watch the want ads carefully. Scan the entire female section, for many jobs can be listed in several different ways. For example, an ad for an editorial assistant may appear under the titles, proofreader, copy editor, gal Friday with editorial know-how, or writer as well as editorial assistant. A secretarial advertisement may appear ubiquitously throughout the entire want ad section as administrative assistant, gal Friday, secretary, executive secretary, clerk-typist with steno or just plain assistant. After you have studied the papers for several weeks, you will become more facile in your detective work. Besides following up want ads, it is often advisable to place an ad in the "situations wanted" column. You can either use a box number or list your telephone. We do suggest that you list your telephone, however, and remain at home for several days to receive phone calls. It is relatively easy to write a small advertisement. Be honest, be concise and state your needs. For example, a secretary just returning to work might develop an ad that sounds like this:

> SECRETARY—mature woman (40) returning to work after fifteen years; excellent steno & typing; adaptable, energetic; Salary Open.
> Box #   Telephone

Professional Agencies

Both state and private agencies are geared to help you meet your job-seeking problems. From these sources, you will be able to ascertain quickly the market conditions, what salary to ask for, and how to approach a particular job situation. Although there is usually a fee involved in the use of private agencies, you will probably find that the agency will attempt to find you a job even where there is no specific opening. There are times when the fee cost will counteract weeks and weeks of job research.

Other Sources

Most colleges have vocational bureaus as placement offices which can give you leads as to where job opportunities may exist. Trade associations and chambers of commerce provide this information too.

Direct Mail Campaign

From the chamber of commerce, you might get a list of the kind of companies you would prefer to work with and conduct your own direct mail campaign. A direct mail campaign is not as overwhelming a task as it may sound. It consists of either a résumé or a letter about yourself. If you intend to use a résumé, be sure that you also enclose a covering letter stating your desires. If you are sending this material out to a number of firms, it is wise to invest in having it mimeographed, multigraphed or offset. Companies no longer demand that every piece of correspondence be hand-typed. The printed résumé is entirely acceptable today. The direct mail campaign can often prove invaluable. One editor whom we know found that she received far more job offers through her own endeavors than she had through all other sources combined.

CHAPTER II | *Tinker, Tailor* . . .

Remember that old nursery rhyme? Choosing a specific job or profession is perhaps a bit more difficult than running your fingers up the buttons of your best dress, but it is not as complicated as it sounds. One of the main decisions that you will have to make concerns timing. You will have to decide *when* to return to the job market, in light of *existing family commitments*. You should ask yourself: Are the children old enough now to permit my going back to work? What effect will the move have on my husband's *modus vivendi?* Can adequate provision be made for household help? Am I willing to take whatever job may be offered me?

If your needs are immediate—if ready cash is a must—you will have to rely on your immediately available skills when you do go back to work. You should by no means let this situation—the fact that for the moment you are in no position to pick and choose—discourage your long-range outlook. Your first back-to-work job can be a pivotal point from which (if bent on a career) you can begin to focus full attention on what you will want to do with the future. There is no reason why a woman cannot work part-time and go to school evenings to gain additional skills.

We know of one woman who, in addition to holding down a full-time job and managing a household, attends college nightly to obtain her B.A. degree. She thrives on this busy schedule. Her philosophy is as follows: "When you're deeply interested in what you're doing, you feel wonderfully stimulated, alive! I'm so busy with projects that I don't have time to be bored. Taking one positive action always seems to produce another, and that one still another. Sometimes I think that fatigue results from nothing more than feeling bored."

When to Look

When the desire to return to the job world is not motivated by dire necessity, you should take the time to ask yourself: "What kind of job will I be happiest in? What area of employment will be the most rewarding to me in terms of emotional and spiritual satisfaction?" In short, since you are in the enviable position of not having to live by bread alone, why not make the most of it? You should analyze these three factors:

1. The requirements of each job.
2. Your qualifications and assets.
3. Your general interests.

Many of the jobs with opportunity, scope and interest are to be found in the professional fields. Are you one of those people who has a B.A. degree? If so, can you afford additional training toward the professional career, for example, of teacher or social worker? The professional occupations, especially in the service areas, are wide open to the mature worker.

FROM KITCHEN TO CAREER

If, however, a professional career seems beyond your grasp, you may want to concentrate on getting an office job. With the current desperate shortage of trained personnel to work as secretaries, stenographers and general office help, any qualified person stands an excellent chance of landing a white-collar job. At Career Blazers we receive many requests for the services of women returning to work. Even if you already have the necessary skills, it is always best to brush up. If you want to learn the skills, there are many schools and institutions which make this training readily available to you.

Find Your Niche

Much of what you ultimately decide to do will probably depend on the education you plan to undertake or have already amassed. Many of the jobs we described have certain educational requirements. If you cannot fulfill the requirements, but are interested in this kind of position, turn to Part II of the book and check whether any of the back-to-school programs would be feasible for you. If you already have a college degree but plan to equip yourself to handle a professional career, you should turn to the Back-to-School chapter and to Chapters VI and XI to determine which careers might be of most interest to you. Should you find a professional career too involving, you might want to check out Chapter VII (The Office Life) or even Chapter IX (A Business of Your Own) and Chapter XI (Careers with the Government). If you have a high school degree and plan to go on to college, be sure to consult the Back-to-School Chapter, the Professional Careers Chapter and the Government Chapter. However, if you can only afford a limited amount of education, also consult Chapters VII, VIII, IX, and X (The Office Life, Develop a Skill, A Business of Your Own, and Spare-Time Dollars).

Knowing your own abilities is, as we have said, highly essential. It is also important that you gear your job-hunting efforts to the realities of your environment. If you live in a large metropolitan area, chances are that a good percentage of the jobs you might aim for are realizable possibilities. If, however, you reside in a small community, the job of your choice may lie a good distance away and thus require you to become a commuter. Before you start spinning your web, be sure that there are flies in the vicinity for you to catch.

Now or Later

We have already touched on the timing of going back to work. One of our favorite people who regularly reports her progress is now engaged in a full-time job as an admitting clerk in a hospital. When she first came to us, she avowed that she would one day be a caseworker, but she said she needed a job desperately—*now*—for her husband had died recently. In view of the fact that she had no skills, but did possess an unusually attractive personality, we suggested work in some service area. We thought of social service or hospitals. She agreed these seemed the most promising since her long-term aim would be furthered by working in this type of atmosphere. Her last report to us was that she had just received her Baccalaureate and won a full-tuition scholarship to graduate school where she would study for her M.A. in social work.

Amazing vitality? Not really. Bear in mind that

Eleanor Roosevelt carried a schedule that would have put the combined effort of two twenty-year-olds to shame practically until the day she died. Mrs. Roosevelt insisted that her interest and enthusiasm were what kept her going. It is a known fact that people possess vast sources of untapped energy. The more you do, the more you *can* do is an old axiom that bears repeating.

Often at Career Blazers we are asked which is the wiser course—immediately taking a job that calls for minimal skills, or going on for further education. Ultimately the decision is up to the individual. Short of intensive analysis, it is difficult to determine which avenue is preferable. We have found, however, that education—like blue-chip-stocks—always pays off. The more educated a person is, the better his job is likely to be. Studies have repeatedly indicated that the college graduate—male and female—receives a consistently higher income than the high school graduate. By the same token, high school graduates receive a higher income than non-high school graduates, except in the case of specialists. There are some fields such as cosmetology, and, of course, a business of your own, where the degree may not matter as much as your ability to sell or promote. But even here, the higher the education, the greater the chance of success.

Look at Your Potential

In estimating your potential, please don't—*do not*—underestimate yourself. Slapping yourself in the face is a lot more harmful and unrealistic than patting yourself on the back. Even women who have worked before sometimes feel that they are too rusty to pick up the thread of their former specialties. Nothing could be further from the truth. Colleges are running special brush-up courses for women who have been out of touch with their professional fields. Educators have found that mathematics majors who haven't cracked a book for as long as fifteen years can be brought up to date in their skills in a matter of months. Finding the right job may seem more difficult if you are a liberal arts graduate or a college drop-out, but don't settle for second best until you have thoroughly explored the possibilities of attaining your first choice. If your dreams tie in with what you can do, give it a try! Two, three, or even four years of college may not be that long a time if you expect to work for the next twenty or thirty.

CHAPTER III | *You*

Now that you have completed the assessment of your present and potential job skills, you are ready for the next step—the assessment of YOU. This is perhaps the more trying evaluation, for we are asking you to appraise how ready you are to meet the emotional demands of the job-seeking situation. The extent of your readiness will be manifested by the answers you give to the following questions:

1. Is my family willing?
2. How do I look?
3. How do I present myself?
4. How do I conduct myself?

Is My Family Willing?

This question poses a large problem. It requires an honest appraisal of just what your role is in your household and whether you can be spared emotionally by the family for outside employment. If your children are pre-school age, you are risking the dilemma of divided responsibilities. It may be difficult for you to concentrate on professional self-improvement when you feel that you have a first duty to your children. If there is no pressing financial necessity to work while they are still very young, a solution to getting out of the house may lie in the area of part-time employment. Another solution may be educational preparation for that time when you will be free to take on a responsible position.

Your husband may also have adverse feelings about your going off to work. If he has been the breadwinner for a number of years, and has become accustomed to prompt dinners, a smooth-running household, and a wife who has been a paragon of devoted service to the various members of the family, he may rebel at the proposed change. Long before you go back to work, it is advisable that you lay the groundwork for family acceptance. Change is easier to swallow if we have been conditioned to it beforehand in easy doses. Going back to work can be a novel, exciting experience, and until you have made it a part of your pattern of life, it can be THE absorbing experience. Your loved ones, though, may only be able to view your absence from hearth and home as a cruel rejection. Thus the woman re-entering the job market after a number of years away from it has a great deal more to consider than does the youngster who is simply training on her first job. The mature woman has already earned a very definite place in society. Chances are that she has made some valuable contributions to her community, is thoughtfully raising her children, and regards her household as a major responsibility. But it is just such a woman who is apt to run into the greatest opposition to her working from the family.

An alteration in the family structure, however, need

not shake the foundations of your home. Gradual indoctrination of the family of the expanding role that modern woman has begun to play in our society will help to crumble resistance. You can also facilitate total adjustment by easing yourself into the position of a working mother, by taking part-time or temporary jobs. Each family is a complex of individual problems, attitudes, likes and dislikes. When a member of the family feels impelled to seek a new challenge, he or she must create a climate that will permit acceptance of the change. Analyze your family's emotional needs and responses even before you study your own. Determine not only when, but also if, going back to work will be feasible. Be honest. Hurt feelings and family stress are a heavy penalty to pay for imperfect timing.

How Do I Look?

Do you look the other way every time you pass the scale? Do your clothes seem to shrink from week to week? Has your hair become dry and withered? No, we are not selling girdles or shampoo—we are back at that old job of appraising.

Anyone who reads a newspaper or magazine, or watches television knows that looking your age does not mean looking like a sack of watermelons. There is absolutely nothing wrong with looking your age. Dignity counts for much more than frills. Well-groomed gray hair can be just as attractive as blazing blond or flaming red, and is far more becoming to the mature in years. A slimmed figure is preferable to a size twenty. A suitable dress is a must.

But let us start at the top and work our way down. It is perfectly all right to color one's hair, provided that the brassy, unnatural colors are avoided. Even youngsters find it difficult to land jobs when their hair heralds their arrival. A becoming hairdo in a color that is suitable to your years and temperament is the first requirement. Whether or not to wear a hat is entirely up to you. If you have the kind of hair that blows wildly in the breeze, a hat helps to keep you looking chic. However, if you feel uncomfortable in a hat, or if your only hats are very dressy, it is better to do without.

Your figure can tell a weighty story about how you have been filling your time—and yourself! You will just have to face it. If you are overweight, you may be in for a problem in getting a job. Acquiring years should not mean getting fat. Less than two percent of the population is afflicted with glandular disorders. Most of the fat accumulated over the past is a direct result of overeating and underexercising. You have probably been telling yourself for some time now the many reasons why you should lose weight. Now you have a major reason. On a purely statistical level, your slim contemporary will get the job nine times out of ten. It is not only that an overweight person is less attractive, but many personnel people feel that overweight is an indication of an emotional problem. A little will power, determination, and a sensible diet will melt the fat right off. Although we cannot promise that a trim figure in itself is the key to getting a job, we can guarantee that your new vigor and appearance will certainly help.

Now that you are svelte, the next item on the agenda is dress. Sloppiness is not accepted at any age, and is unforgivable in the mature woman. (Companies often feel that a youngster will outgrow her slatternly habits as she becomes more conscious of being a woman, but in the mature woman the case is usually considered hopeless.) Wear clothes that are becoming; clothes that are comfortable. Remember the outfit that you choose should be one in which you can spend at least ten hours and still feel comfortable. Overdressing is as bad as underdressing. A cocktail dress is in as bad taste as a house dress. One candidate who we felt had fine potential was turned down, interview after interview. Although she had gone back to school to secure her degree in math, her appearance was unfortunately so dowdy that she looked more like a cleaning woman than a professional. A simple dark dress or suit, hat and gloves, and comfortable medium-heeled shoes compose a good starting formula. If you do not happen to have this kind of outfit, treat yourself to one. We assure you that it will pay for itself. Many housewives find that although they have an ample supply of slacks, shifts, housedresses and evening wear, they have no clothes suitable for business.

Be careful about your shoes. Many women who have reached middle age find that they can no longer wear as lofty a heel as they did in their youth. It is definitely not necessary to wear high, spiked heels to complete your outfit if you are uncomfortable in them. When you are looking for a job, you are bound to do a lot of walking. That footsore feeling cannot only mar your interview, but may also keep you home the next few days, wasting valuable time. On the other hand, an absolutely flat playshoe, no matter how comfortable, is also to be avoided. If this is the only kind of shoe you can wear, it is better to carry a pair of pumps in a small bag and change your shoes when you go out on an interview.

YOU

Vis-a-Vis—Or How Do I Present Myself?

This involves the face-to-face interview, the letter of application, and the résumé. All contribute to making up the total YOU. Each must be presented in a unique manner; it is your validity as a person which breathes vitality into each facet and makes them convincing to a prospective employer.

The Interview

The initial interview should not be viewed with alarm. If you feel trepidation at the prospect, rest assured that you are in good company. Of the thousands of people we have interviewed at Career Blazers, a common bond unites them—dislike and fear of the interview. One young woman dramatically stated, "I would rather have a tooth filled without novocain, than go to an interview." It is amazing how many applicants don't keep their interview appointments. The percentage of delinquents has been estimated as high as twenty-five percent and the number of late arrivers is said to range from 50 to 65 percent. No matter what the percentage, we are convinced that the ones who don't "show" are not insincere applicants neglectful of the value of other people's time, but rather individuals who suddenly pale at what faced them and develop good old-fashioned "cold feet." At times it may take will power and discipline to keep an appointment when every little fear wave is amplified into a crescendo of "Go home, tomorrow's another day." If going to an interview seems like having your teeth pulled, remember—the same self-discipline and determination that got you to your dentist are what steel you to attend your first job interview.

Actually, if we examine the interview procedure in

the clear light of reason, it loses much of its terror. It is not a path leading to the guillotine, nor is it a subtle inquisition to undermine your sense of worth—it consists merely of two persons meeting to determine qualifications and discuss the job in question. Always remember, it works both ways. It is just as important for the company to sell itself to you as it is for you, the applicant, to sell yourself to the company. What the job seeker may not realize is clear to us from our perspective—many a company has lost the applicant it wants because its offer was not as attractive as that of another company. The organization needs and wants qualified people as desperately as the applicant needs and wants a good job. Naturally, the personnel manager of the company does seem to have an advantage since he or she already has a job and, in representing the company, has a more specific knowledge of what is necessary to fill the position. However, bear in mind that you, in turn, have a specific talent to "sell." You would not be looking for a job with this organization if you did not have certain qualifications which it is seeking.

The Agelessness of Truth!

Our experience at Career Blazers has proved to us again and again that sincerity is the most effective approach in job hunting. It is more comfortable to be direct. Give yourself that comfort. If you are fifty, be fifty. While it is legally permissible to list yourself as "twenty-one plus" on your application, you are only inviting guessing games and confusion. You might *look* any age from forty to sixty. A "twenty-one plus" may induce the personnel manager to figure you on the high side of fifty rather than on the low side. It is against the law to discriminate for reasons of age. More and more, companies are trying to absorb mature women into their hiring picture. And while certain trainee programs are best suited to younger, and more recent graduates, other programs require the special talents that only experience can offer. Respect the company's decision as to the department in which you might be happiest. If there is no immediate opening, there is a possibility that something might open in the next few weeks. A successful interview can land you a job in the near future as well as on the day of the interview.

"Speech Is Silver—Silence Golden"

What you say is as important as what you wear! If you bear in mind that an interview is merely a meeting between you and the personnel department to determine if and how you can benefit each other, you will soon lose your interview "jitters." Answer as honestly and unemotionally as possible. Be brief. The personnel manager is really not interested in your life story. Be positive. Questions such as why you want to go back to work should be answered directly and firmly. We assume that before you face your first interview you have examined your motives for returning to work quite thoroughly. Such answers as "I'm bored at home," "Work has always fascinated me," "I want to find myself," "I want to be creative," etc., do not impress a personnel manager. Even some of the most stimulating jobs entail a great deal of clerical drudgery. Phrases like the above lead the personnel manager to assume that you will not be interested in performing the detail. On the other hand, lowering yourself to the level of "I'll

FROM KITCHEN TO CAREER

do anything," "I'll sweep floors," etc., is also insincere. You won't sweep floors and you know it.

The profit motive is always a sensible reason for going back to work. The need to re-enter the business world to lead a fuller, more constructive life makes good sense. Remember that the company is trying to find out what you can do for it, and although the company is willing to pay you a salary commensurate to work performance, it is not willing to be your psychiatrist. By the time you are looking for work, you should have your emotional needs under control.

There are so many factors that operate in obtaining a job. Recently at Career Blazers, we were working with a client who specified that he needed a mature woman to handle a responsible position in the company library. The job required voluminous reading of magazines and newspapers to ferret out facts that would be of interest to the company and later to organize these facts into a small library. We searched our files and came up with the following three candidates:

> Mrs. R., age forty-five, had three years of college and had worked as a receptionist-clerical assistant while her husband was in medical school. Recently she had worked as a library assistant in a non-profit foundation.
> Mrs. B., age forty-seven, was an avid reader. Her daughters were now in college and she was anxious to return to the business world. She had neither a college education nor any recent experience. Her only job immediately after high school had been a simple filing one.
> Mrs. J. seemed the most likely candidate of the three. She was forty, had a bachelor's degree in English from an Ivy League college and her Master's degree in philosophy. She had handled a small library in connection with her other duties as an administrative assistant to a research editor of a publishing company. Her experience was recent and her capabilities were proven.

We assumed that Mrs. J. was the woman for the job. If she did not work out, we believed that Mrs. R. then would be a good choice. We set up an appointment, first for Mrs. J., then Mrs. R., and we encouraged the personnel interviewer also to see Mrs. B., mainly because of Mrs. B.'s strong desire to work. After a week of interviews and discussions, Mrs. B. was hired!

Why? Mrs. B. wanted the job, and was willing to go to school to learn more about the work she would be doing. Her manner and charm were exceptional. It is interesting to diagnose what Mrs. B. did that the other two more-qualified women did not do.

Reversing the usual procedure, Mrs. J. interviewed the personnel manager! He reported back to us that she immediately took charge of the meeting. She interrogated him as to salary increases, bonus, vacations, coffee breaks, etc. She told him she believed the company should pay the agency fee and questioned him about the methods used in picture filing in the library. She disapproved of the stated method and immediately outlined a new system. Her aggressiveness was out of bounds. She was domineering, non-feminine, and in the personnel manager's word, "arrogant."

Mrs. R. handled the first interview with decorum. She was asked to come back to meet the vice-president. For some reason, she took this as an encouragement to talk freely, and, on meeting him, launched into a confession. She became very cosy and intimate, confiding that she must get a job, that this job seemed as good as any, that the staff seemed warm and friendly, that she must get away from home since her mother-in-law visited her every day and was driving her mad. This woman raved on and on, using up an executive's valuable time and talking herself right out of a job.

Mrs. B., on the other hand, seems to have struck the right formula. She let the interviewer lead the interview. Although she appeared somewhat shy at the beginning, she was nevertheless cheerful and optimistic. She answered all the questions in a courteous, straightforward manner. She offered to take courses at night. She demonstrated a sincere interest and willingness to do what she could to make herself useful to the company. The interviewer felt that what Mrs. B. did not know, she could easily learn. He also felt that her lack of experience would in no way hamper her but might, in fact, act as an incentive for her to learn the job more thoroughly.

Do's and Don'ts

A good general rule to bear in mind when on an interview is to be courteous, and aware of what is in good taste. Decorum, dignity and honesty should be the guidelines. To help you further in your job campaign, the following list of do's and don'ts has been found successful:

> Do ALWAYS BE ON TIME. If a delay is unavoidable, be sure to phone the personnel manager and re-schedule your interview.
>
> Do WAIT PATIENTLY if the personnel manager cannot get to you on time. He or she is aware of your crowded schedule, but emergencies do arise. If you find yourself becoming hostile, ask the receptionist to re-schedule you at a more convenient time. Stewing around will not make a good impression.
>
> Do COMPLETE THE ENTIRE APPLICATION BLANK. Even if you have to search your memory for facts and

dates, try to put them down. It is wise before you start your job search to go back into your files for pertinent facts such as dates of education, of places worked, and, if possible, the names of your immediate supervisors each time. Keep these facts on a handy 3 x 5 card and use it as a reference. We have been told that one of the reasons a job is not offered is that the application card is inaccurately or incorrectly filled out.

DO APPEAR INTERESTED. Be alert and uncomplicated. Do discuss the present job opening, not where it will lead in five years.

DO BE POISED AND CHARMING. Remember that being nervous does not indicate want of poise. Personnel managers are quite prepared for the nervous applicant. They know that the jitters will disappear. They also know that arrogance and lack of humility will generally increase once the individual is on the job, and that these traits are much more unacceptable than nervousness or timidity.

DO BE POSITIVE. Keep your spirits high. Fortunately, courage and enthusiasm are contagious. But, unfortunately, so are gloom and pessimism. A cheerful attitude is an asset, a gloomy one, a severe debit.

DO HAVE A REASONABLY GOOD IDEA OF WHAT YOU WANT TO DO. Throwing your problem into the lap of the interviewer only serves to backfire against your chances of success. You are right back where you started with one less prospect of a job.

DON'T BE RUDE. Rudeness includes not showing up for an interview, being late, interrupting, using slang, chewing gum, taking notes while someone is talking, telling the interviewer that he does not know his job, walking out in the middle of an interview, blowing smoke in the interviewer's face, pulling your chair so close that he moves back in self-defense, becoming intimate and cosy, etc.

DON'T DO ANYTHING IN EXCESS. Don't overdress, don't underdress; don't be aggressive, don't be a mouse, don't be too formal, don't be a coy mistress, don't itch to leave, don't overstay, don't drown your interview in chatter, don't pull the drawbridge down over your mouth. As the ancient Greeks advised, practice moderation.

DON'T TAKE OFFENSE if the personnel manager is younger than yourself. Age has little to do with competency. He or she is placed there by the organization because of his or her special qualifications to represent the company.

DON'T FEEL THAT YOU HAVE TO BE INTERVIEWED BY A MAN. A female interviewer is not hostile to other women. She is seeking to fill the position with the most qualified applicant she can find. If you are not suited for that particular job, don't blame it on her age or her sex. A good interview may land you another job in the company several weeks hence. Don't spoil it by becoming hostile if you do not get the job for which you are interviewing.

DON'T BE DISCOURAGED! If you feel the pangs, snap out of it. Discouragement is a luxury. We learned this from the experience of an applicant we tried to place several years ago. He had once held a very high position in the government. He was accused of a heinous crime, tried and sentenced. When he was released from prison, he began looking for a job—any job, even a fifty dollar-a-week stock room position. Month after month, he courageously combed the city looking for a company willing to forget the unpleasant past and help him to create a future. We suffered right along with him the agonies of his situation, and one day we finally asked him if he were not discouraged. We have never forgotten the courageous, almost defiant look on his face when he answered, "Discouragement is a luxury I cannot afford."

The Resume:

Whether you have a great deal or just a few words to say about yourself and your work experience, remember that your résumé will present a word picture of you. In essence, a good résumé is merely a simple, realistic statement of truth about yourself. Don't balk at preparing a résumé, even if you feel that you have nothing to say. As you start thinking about what you have done in the past ten or twenty years, you may find that some of your volunteer work will lend itself to various job categories. In painting a picture of yourself in words, it is useful to prepare an inventory. First, list on a sheet of paper all of your education. Be sure to include adult education courses, college courses (even those which are non-matriculated) as well as university extension courses. Second, list all the paid work experience you have had. Include those jobs you held during your earlier years. Include all the part-time jobs you have held. Third, list all of the posts you have held in volunteer work. Delve deeply for special project activity. Fourth, list any special skills and hobbies you have acquired.

Now that you've put yourself down on paper, you have a pool of information from which to draw. Keep these sheets handy so that when you apply for a job you can fill out application blanks with much more ease. For example, if you are applying for a job as secretary in a non-profit organization, you probably will find that your "selling posture" is enhanced by the fact that you have been active in volunteer organizations involved in a similar project. The fact that you have taken courses in a field related to the job in question would also increase the possibility of your getting the job.

In preparing the résumé, keep it brief and to the point. Since much of your life experience can be directed in any number of ways, we suggest that you prepare a résumé for each type of job rather than fashion a broad outline that does not pin-point your activity. Suppose that, although you have gone back to school to get graduate degrees for professional work, you still want to get a job as a secretary for a short time before pursuing your professional career. In this instance, you would underplay your graduate work and emphasize your skills. If you are seeking a part-time job while studying for a professional career, you would place the emphasis on skills and demonstration of work ability.

Long-range career aspirations are not required information in a résumé. The company is interested in what you can do for it NOW, and not what you want to be. Declaring your dreams is the "kiss of death."

Use standard size bond paper. Try to use the white space effectively. Keep the writing style simple. Avoid "gimmick" résumés as much as possible. Cuteness might be (but almost never is) acceptable in the young "junior," but in the mature woman, it is unforgivable. Include your name, address and telephone number in a conspicuous place. Give dates on repetitive schooling, jobs and volunteer activities. When listing references, be sure the persons involved are aware that you are using their names. A surprise call from a prospective employer can sometimes be embarrassing. Don't expect a mailed reply to your résumé when the company's answer is negative. Many personnel offices do try to reply to every piece of correspondence they receive, but often the task is insurmountable.

If you have had very little or no work experience, a typical résumé might read as follows:

Mrs. Jane Doe	Married
111 Tremont St.	Two Children
Battle Creek, Michigan	Richard, age 17
	Marilyn, age 15

TELEPHONE: PO 8-5463
POSITION DESIRED: Secretary
EDUCATION: St. Mary's High School, 1942
               University of Detroit, 1942-1944
WORK EXPERIENCE:
       Assisted husband in his business one or two days a week, as the situation required.
       Answered telephone inquiries, handled correspondence, and kept the books.
VOLUNTEER EXPERIENCE:
       Secretary, PTA, 1950-55
       Secretary-Treasurer, United Community Funds and Councils, 1959-63
SPECIAL SKILLS:
       Completed a one-year course in shorthand and typing at La Salle Business School, 1964
       Shorthand—120 words per minute
       Typing—60 words per minute

This is all you need to put into a résumé of this kind. More information would be extraneous. You are going after a secretarial position, and you indicate that 1) you are familiar with office procedure through working in your husband's office; 2) you have held responsible volunteer positions; and 3) you have taken the trouble to learn, or to brush up on, the skills that will be needed for this job. By giving the children's ages, you also indicate that your children are old enough to take care of themselves. There is no need to explain why you want to go to work. The information that you have included on a résumé of this kind is an explanation in itself.

Now let us assume you are a woman who had a secretarial career before the birth of your child. Now that you have earned a degree qualifying you for professional work, your résumé might be formulated as follows:

Mrs. Ruth Summers
44 Broadcast Lane
Phoenix, Arizona

Married:
3 children:
Catherine, age 19
Mary, age 14
JoAnne, age 10

POSITION DESIRED: Elementary Teacher
EDUCATION:
    B.A., Philosophy, New York University, 1941
    M.A., Early Childhood Education,
        University of Arizona, 1964
VOLUNTEER WORK:
    Chairman, PTA, 1955-1960
    Treasurer, PTA, 1952-1955
    Chairman, PTA, Special Activities, 1950-1952
    Chairman, Red Cross Drive, 1954-1956
    Special Events Chairman, Junior Hadassah, 1945-1954

WORK EXPERIENCE:
    Editorial Assistant, 1941-1943
    Double Publishing Company
    55 East 60 St.
    New York, N. Y.

SPECIAL INTERESTS AND HOBBIES:
    Camping, skating, fishing, classical music, extensive reading.

SPECIAL ACHIEVEMENTS:
    Have written and illustrated a children's book which is currently being considered for publication.

Note that everything in the résumé indicates an interest in working with people and children. You know what you want to do, and your background indicates without question that you can probably do the job. All you need now is the interview.

Keep the stuffing out of a résumé. It goes with roast chicken but not with job hunting! If you follow the general outline of these two résumés, adding or subtracting where you see fit, you cannot go wrong.

Letter of Application. If you are answering a box number or a newspaper advertisement, a letter of application is more advisable than a formal résumé. Simply incorporate into the body of the letter all the information that is pertinent. Proofread it carefully to make sure there are no grammatical or spelling errors. Many a job has been lost because a would-be editor or secretary misspelled a word. Letters that depend on trick effects are facetious and should be avoided. A postcard stating that you would like more information about the job before applying is usually discarded on receipt.

The same rules hold for the written word as for the job interview. In the letter, you are representing yourself. Put your best foot forward and hope for a favorable reaction. The fewer games you play, the more response you are likely to receive.

Be realistic! When you apply for a job through a newspaper ad, evaluate whether or not you have the qualifications. A job may look great and you may feel there is no reason why you cannot handle it. But if you equate twenty years of running a house with a job requiring administration at a ten-thousand-dollar level, you are way off base. You're only wasting paper and postage and exposing your naïveté. Although you are mature, balanced and adaptable, you will still have to learn new procedures.

ORGANIZE your job-hunting routine. Keep records of the letters you send out, the names of personnel managers and employment agents you have visited. Jot down the time of each appointment and note the success or failure of each interview. When you are especially interested in a job, send off a short note of thanks to the personnel manager. Keep your interviews to a reasonable number per day. If you find that you can do only two interviews in one day, keep it down to two. It is better to arrive fresh for two interviews than to try to cram in as many as possible. If you are in a big city, get a street map and try to arrange your interviews in one section of the city at a time. This will save you considerable emotional and financial wear-and-tear.

CHAPTER IV | *Testing*

When you finally pass muster on the letter of application, the résumé, appearance and personal interview, you may find yourself faced with still another hurdle—the test. This may range from a short skill test to a battery of aptitude and psychological tests that can last as long as one or two days. *Do not be alarmed.* Just as we have reached the plastic age in material goods, we have reached the testing age in determining a person's ability. But keep in mind, the tests given are neither that difficult nor that terrifying. They are not like the tests you took in the classroom when if you had not read your history you failed. Most tests are supplemental to the interview, and not meant to put you on trial. They are designed to elicit information about your aptitudes and interests, and only given if the personnel manager feels there is a good chance of hiring you.

Skill Tests

Let us begin with the simple skill tests used in typing or secretarial placement. The test is not given to put you on the spot—it often uncovers a potentially good skill. The typing test is simple. You are given several paragraphs to type and are timed on how many words per minute you can do. For each error you make, ten words are subtracted from the total. For example, if you type sixty words per minute and you make three errors, your net typing speed is thirty words per minute. It is always better to type more slowly and be accurate than to attempt speed and risk lowering your average. You can test yourself at home by using a time clock and typing news items from the paper. Always use new material when you try yourself—otherwise you are not giving yourself a fair test.

The stenography test is similar to the typing test. A person dictates a letter or several paragraphs to you. You take down the material in shorthand and are asked either to read the material back or transcribe it from your notes. Generally, the steno speed required is between eighty and ninety words per minute. For a beginner, the expert speeds of one hundred and twenty or better are not demanded. You can also practice rusty steno at home by trying to take down speeches and news broadcasts from the radio. It is better at first to have a friend dictate letters to you, and then, as you gain experience, increase the tempo. Again we caution that you do not try for speed immediately. Accuracy here is as important as in typing, for a word missed can change the entire structure of a letter. We know of a stenographer who transcribed a "new defect" into a "nude effect." The response was electric, but unfortunately the young lady was fired.

Figure Aptitude

Figure aptitude can be tested in many ways. You

may be given some figures to post from one column to another, or you may be given a short clerical test that will involve addition and subtraction. Usually, if the job is clerical, a figure aptitude test will not demand any greater skill than average adding and subtracting and the ability to transpose figures from one sheet to another. Some people cannot copy figures correctly and this becomes a serious handicap in any job involving figures. Certain tests will expose this inability.

Intelligence Tests

Intelligence tests vary from a simple four-page test to the complicated Stanford-Binet IQ test. It is unusual to be tested by the Stanford-Binet method since this involves the time of a psychologist. More than likely you will be given a small intelligence test that will determine to some extent your verbal and motor skills. Don't let it throw you. If you have been helping Junior with his homework, or budgeting the family dollar, you will probably pass with flying colors.

To allay your fears, see if you can answer some of the following questions:

A. DO THE WORDS *MINER—MINOR* HAVE
   1. Similar meanings. 2. Contradictory.
   3. Neither.

B. How many of the items listed below are exact duplicates of each other?

545	545
910043	919043
3322042	3320042
385002215	385002215

C. Assume that the first two statements are true. Is the final one (1) true, (2) false, (3) not certain? These puppies are normal dogs. All normal dogs are playful. These puppies are playful.

The answers to these three questions are as follows:
A—3
B—2
C—1

As you can see, these tests are quite simple. However, the more complicated the job for which you interview, the more complex will be the test.

Tests for College Entrance

Tests in the academic world are different from those used by industry. For example, if you decide to enter college, you may find that you will be required to take the same college boards that junior and senior high school students are taking. Unfortunately, some colleges do not recognize that in the intervening years much superficial knowledge is lost. If that is the case, it may be wise to take some refresher courses in your local high school to help you pass the boards. The most difficult areas for people untrained in the sciences are in mathematics. Verbal skills usually improve with age. It is worth the time to brush up on your algebra and geometry if it means passing a test.

If you do not pass the first time—no matter what the test is—try again if it is at all possible! Many personnel interviewers understand that the individual may have been nervous and do take this into consideration. They are also very impressed when an applicant asks for a second chance at a test. Never be afraid to ask for a warm-up period on a typing or steno test. Again, bear in mind that you are not on trial. Testing is merely to determine how much you know and where you will be most valuable to the firm.

Vocational Guidance

Should you feel that you need preparation and direction before embarking on a job career, you may want to turn to professional guidance. In most large cities you will find both private and public vocational guidance bureaus. Very often, the college in your vicinity will also have facilities for testing and guidance. For more information, write for the Directory of Vocational Counseling Services, published by the American Personnel and Guidance Association, 1605 New Hampshire Avenue, N.W., Washington 9, D.C.

Usually when you apply for guidance and counseling, one of the first steps is to participate in a battery of psychological tests. These tests measure abilities or aptitudes in the following areas: intelligence and learning ability, verbal aptitude, numerical aptitude, spatial aptitude, form perception, clerical perception, motor coordination, finger dexterity and manual dexterity. When the results of your tests have been scored, the counselor will discuss with you the work areas in which you are likely to be most successful.

One word of warning, however! Often the counselor is not apprised of the job market. If your aptitudes are strongest in music, for example, and there is no market for a music major, the counseling will turn out to be flattering but non-productive. If you do have yourself vocationally tested, be sure that your career choice lies within the realm of possibility. An expensive education that leads to a dead-end should be avoided.

PART TWO

CHAPTER V | *Back To School*

Esse paratis. Be prepared. Join the thousands of women going back to school to learn a skill, a profession, or just to learn! If you want to go back to work in dignity and style, chuck the afternoon teas for afternoon seminars. Housewives on the campus know the delight of that alive, brain-stretching feeling that comes with learning and self-growth.

The insistent call for and need of the housewife who grows younger and more beautiful as she matures is finally being met by a number of forward-looking colleges. Since brides and grooms in the last decade have blossomed younger and younger, and since child-bearing has been a function of the teens and early twenties, the woman in her late twenties, thirties or forties may find herself with time on her hands. Freed by modern technology, by improved physical health and by such writers as Betty Friedan in her *The Feminine Mystique,* the housewife who has interrupted her education to marry and raise a family will probably be casting about for some kind of meaningful work. Often (if she is still far from forty) the work that will be of greatest interest to her will be in professional areas.

And—she is now aided and abetted in planning a career based on greater education and knowledge. Thomas Jefferson once said that "the fate of a nation depends upon the education of its people," and those in the know (our educators, sociologists, economists, political scientists and other leaders of society) include all women as part of the nation. Aware that intelligent women who do not work have become a source of latent talent and power, those in government are expressing a desire and concern that just such women be encouraged toward productive careers.

Psychologists parallel governmental thinking, but their main concern is that the woman grow, expand and function in a work society as an antidote to after-40-blues.

Liberal Arts Institutions

As a result of this dynamic change in attitude about women, we have found that the colleges are opening their campuses to the mature diploma-seeker. We predict that this is only the beginning. By the time this book is completed, many more colleges will have climbed aboard the bandwagon. There will be many more progressive plans to get the woman back into the market. The rest is up to you!

The colleges which at this writing are actively engaged in educating the mature woman are: Douglass College, Sarah Lawrence College, The University of Minnesota, Boston University Division of Continuing Education, University of Oklahoma, Boston College, Brooklyn College of New York, Queens College, Simmons College, Tufts University, Wellesley College,

BACK TO SCHOOL

Northeastern University, Radcliffe College, Goddard College Institute for Independent Study, Harvard Graduate School of Education. If a college near your town or city has not been mentioned, do not despair. Since these pilot programs, which we shall describe, have proved so successful, colleges all over the country are taking notice and instituting similar programs which soon may be available in your locale. Check with your nearest college. You may be a charter member in its back-to-school movement.

University of Minnesota

The Minnesota plan for continuing the education of women is one of the most extensive. This is one of the college plans that is sponsored by the Carnegie Corporation. Its entrance requirements ask no more of a woman than that she have a strong intellectual curiosity and an ability to do college work. There "on-campus-counselors" help the "returnee" decide on her course of study so that it will fit in with the time she has to give. Gone is the rigidity of the undergraduate teenage problems. Now the mature woman with her life problems is treated with dignity and respect, and is helped in every way possible to overcome household handicaps that may stand in the way of her getting a degree. Scholarships and nursery care are an integrated part of the program. A variety of course study is offered including evening classes, day sessions, radio and TV sessions, refresher courses, neighborhood seminars, home study (the University will send an instructor to homes for a group of sixteen or more). Alert to a growing nation with ever-increasing needs, the University of Minnesota's goals are quite simple but remarkably penetrating. It hopes to make the best possible use of our country's most valuable asset—its educated women. The University of Minnesota does this by helping the individual woman to realize her intellectual or professional goal. It's that simple.

How do the women respond? The University's program at this writing is only three years old, and already some fifteen hundred "rusty" women have been counseled or directed into a course of study. The distinguishing feature of the Minnesota plan is its flexibility. The plan is characterized as follows: "It is not a college or institution, it has no course of study; rather it is an advisory and coordinating service concerned with the broad range of educational problems of women."* It is interested in the woman from eighteen to eighty at whatever level of education.

In the 1942 newsletter of the Minnesota plan, a number of scholarship winners are described. One woman, age forty-seven, after adopting and raising two sons, lost her husband. She sold the farm, moved to Minneapolis and attended a short-term medical technician school to gain immediate employment for a long-term scientific career. Another woman, age thirty-five, must support her seven children, ages six to fifteen. She returned to school after sixteen years, having saved enough money to take five credits. Proving to herself that she could do it, she earned the scholarship and now has twenty-one credits toward a Speech Pathology career. Another woman, fifty-three, has been accepted into a new graduate program at the University. She is in a program that will combine the fields of home eco-

* The Carnegie Corp. of N.Y., *Quarterly*, Oct. 16, 1962, Vol. X, No. 4.

nomics, sociology and social work. This is a program that was developed by the Health and Welfare Section of the American Home Economics Association, and this woman is one of the first to be accepted for the program. She is making a sacrifice to attend, for she leaves her husband and sixteen-year-old daughter for five days each week to attend the sessions.

Radcliffe

Radcliffe, another college participating in the Carnegie Plan, is more rigorous and selective than those we have already mentioned. Its Institute for Independent Study gives grants up to $3,000 a year to gifted and accomplished women who are interested in graduate study or in creative work. It is only open to those who already have a degree. Twenty scholars were chosen during the first year of the program from among several hundred applicants. All but two of these women had advanced degrees. Only one woman had just a B.A., and the other, an accomplished poet, did not have any degree. The ages ranged from the late twenties to the early fifties. All but one were married. They had from one to four children.

The scholar in the Radcliffe plan was allowed to work on any project she chose. She could avail herself of all the facilities of the University—laboratories, libraries, study rooms at either Radcliffe or Harvard. She could attend the weekly seminars at Cambridge and present her work for criticism and discussion. The results were exceedingly productive. During the year, nine students of the Institute either had their writings published or were in preparation to publish; another had given two piano concerts; an artist had a "one-man" show.

FROM KITCHEN TO CAREER

Oklahoma

In the spring of 1961, Thurman White, Dean of the University of Oklahoma's Extension Division, introduced a Bachelor of Liberal Studies program for adults. The pilot group of one hundred and fifty people, ranging in age from twenty-three to seventy, has already proven the worth of this program. Only a year and a half in existence, the program already boasts eight members who have earned their degrees. The success of this unique program is attributable to its placing the adult at his own level of attainment. It is geared to the student, operating on the theory that the shoe must be fitted to the foot, not vice-versa. Admission to the program requires that the student have a high school degree or an equivalent certificate.

Since the Oklahoma Plan's degree is based on broad areas of study such as the humanities, the social sciences, and the natural sciences, a large part of the program can be completed in special area study programs. Only thirteen weeks of residence study are required to attain the degree; independent study, four seminars, and extensive examinations are substituted for the usual academic program. The total cost runs between thirteen hundred and fifteen hundred dollars, plus living expenses during the seminars. There are also supplemental programs and weekend residential programs that B.L.S. students may find useful.

For more information write to the College of Continuing Education, The University of Oklahoma, Norman, Oklahoma.

Sarah Lawrence

At Sarah Lawrence, the program is limited to women who have had at least one year of college work, want to earn a degree, and who live in the greater New York area. Mainly, the Center serves the woman who needs help in selecting the course of study best suited to herself and her family's needs. The Center is concerned with advising her as to the best facilities available and encouraging the creation of educational programs to meet her need. The Center itself has a program in operation that is now limited to fifteen students. It meets for one long session a week, and provides individual conferences each week or in alternate weeks. Students are, of course, expected to do a great deal of work on their own. After taking this "warm-up" for a semester or a year, the student may then apply for matriculation at Sarah Lawrence and take the courses that she needs for her particular major. Sarah Lawrence tries to meet and accommodate the needs of this special group. For more information, write to Mrs. Esther Raushenbush, Director of Sarah Lawrence College's New Center for the Continuing Education of Women, Bronxville, New York.

Goddard College

Goddard's plan may be the perfect answer to the interrupted college career. Founded twenty-five years ago, Goddard is located in Plainfield, Vermont. Always progressive, stressing the development of independent thinking and responsibility, the college is now concentrating on adult education. Since its inception, Goddard has always welcomed the few adults who could continue with full-time college study. However, the college has been aware that many adults simply are unable to pack up and move to Plainfield, Vermont, to continue a college education, no matter how great the need or desire.

FROM KITCHEN TO CAREER

Therefore, Goddard inaugurated what we feel may turn out to be the complete answer to mature needs—one of the most revolutionary plans for adults ever created. The Goddard scheme combines week-long resident seminars with a six-month period of individual and independent study. The seminars include lectures, discussions and conferences with staff members. This is the "set-up" for the work ahead. The student during the following six months keeps in touch with the faculty through correspondence, telephone conferences, exchange of tape recordings and monthly newsletters. There are also progress reports by the students, regional meetings with faculty members, and short visits to the campus if location permits. The six-month independent study period is followed by another week on campus for evaluation and preparation for the next cycle. This study is geared to cover a complete liberal arts program including history, government, literature, natural science, anthropology, etc.

The program is open to men and women who have completed at least two semesters of satisfactory college work, have been out of college for at least five years, and are at least twenty-six years old. The student must also be able to spend the two-week period on the Vermont campus. During the "on campus" weeks, conferences and aptitude tests will be held to help the student not only toward college success, but also eventual job placement.

Essentially, each six-month cycle is the equivalent of a college semester. With the completion of the required cycles, the student earns his B.A. degree. Costs are less than at the average college, and it is estimated that a student with two years of successful college study might be able to complete his degree for about three thousand dollars.

For further information, write to: The Adult Degree Program at Goddard College, Plainfield, Vermont.

Brooklyn College

In 1951, the Fund for Adult Education, sponsored by the Ford Foundation, established a grant for universities that were seeking to initiate or improve liberal education programs for adults. Many of the universities used this money to help the adult obtain a broader perspective on the humanities and social sciences through a series of discussion programs. Other schools, of which Brooklyn College is a prime example, developed a program by which an adult could receive a Baccalaureate degree at night with a minimum of expense and time.

This program is perhaps one of the most outstanding now in operation. The first two years of study comprise two seminars, one in the humanities and the other in the social sciences. The student attends only two evenings a week. The humanities seminar is twelve credits' worth of work, completed in two semesters and totaling twenty-four credits; the social sciences, eight credits each semester, totaling sixteen credits. Credits from other colleges are transferable and accepted wherever possible. Special tutorials are set up for courses that a student feels he can handle primarily on his own. Life experience is evaluated in the form of credits. For example, a student who had been active in modern dance was granted eight credits from the dance department. Another student who had had an extensive theatrical career before attending the program was granted fifteen credits from the speech and drama department. The average number of credits for life experience varies between thirty and forty, but one student is known to have been granted fifty credits.

This program also allows a student to major in whatever field he or she feels is best suited to his interests. There are no limits set. Special teachers who understand the problem of the adult going back to school are provided during the seminar years. Special counseling is also furnished to guide the adult into the most effective course structure.

The majority of both men and women students are married, and most have children, some of whom are already in college. One woman, a grandmother, was fulfilling a life-long ambition to go to college. Another woman employed in a special school for emotionally disturbed children found that in order to continue her service, it would be necessary for her to get a degree. She, therefore, enrolled in the program. There were two secretaries in the class who wanted to teach, two widows who at the age of forty were faced with having to redesign their life-plan. Because our highly specialized society requires re-training, these people found college to be their only answer.

By June, 1962, of the total number of graduates of the Brooklyn College program, fifty-four had achieved honors: nine, *summa cum laude;* thirteen, *magna cum laude;* and thirty-two, *cum laude.* Forty-nine have gone on to various graduate schools. Twelve graduates have received their Master's degree, and four are candidates for the Ph.D. Several graduates have received scholarships.

Admission to the program requires that the applicant fill out an application blank, take a graduate record examination, and have a personal interview. As education prices go, the costs of the entire program are relatively inexpensive. Tuition for the first two years runs about one thousand dollars. The tutorial service costs twenty dollars per credit; independent reading for each course, twenty dollars; evaluation of life experience, fifty dollars. If the student lives within metropolitan New York, he can matriculate for the remainder of his credits, thus taking advantage of New York City's free educational system.

With the success of the Brooklyn program, other universities have begun to consider the advisability of seting up a pilot adult division. In 1963, Queens College instituted its first seminar patterned after the Brooklyn example. This concept is so new that even as you read this book, several colleges and possibly one in your own vicinity may be making plans of this nature. As one graduate wrote in the *Harvard Education Review* (Spring, 1962):

> There is a cadre of mature adults in every urban center; men and women lacking college degrees, dissatisfied with the haphazard adult education courses offered by almost all "in town" institutions. These "extension" or "non-credit" courses have no unity or purpose. Attending such classes may be preferable, to reasonably intelligent, mature adults, to watching the inanities of television, but they fail to stimulate a drive for a goal, without which studying becomes sporadic and usually dies on the vine.

Rutgers

Ever watchful for new educational possibilities, the Ford Foundation developed in 1961 a program for the retraining of mature women in the field of mathematics. The Rutgers plan came into being because of a survey that revealed two important facts: industry would hire mature women who had a background in new mathematical concepts, and mature women were definitely interested in returning to school for retraining in a specially developed mathematical program. The Rutgers program has been so successful that it is presently being expanded into the field of chemistry. Students are often offered jobs in both teaching and industry before they have finished their course work. Job requests often remain unfilled at Career Blazers until a graduate comes fresh from school, equipped with newly-acquired qualifications.

The program is open to any woman or man who has had some college math. Pioneer of the far-seeing plan is Mrs. Helen Marston, a lecturer in math at Douglass College (the women's division of Rutgers). In 1961, its first year, Douglass enrolled fifty-three women. The average student was forty-one, in an age range of twenty-five to sixty-nine. Of a total of one hundred and thirty-two women enrolled to date, one hundred and twenty-five are married, with an average of 2.8 children. People commute from as far away as Port Washington, New York and Philadelphia.

The job score is high. Twenty of the alumni are already teaching, with an average salary of $5,000. Two are in college teaching. Fourteen are working in industry or research with an average salary of about $6,000. Seven went on to graduate school and seven are doing substitute teaching. The women who have attended the Rutgers program are indeed setting an inspiring example. One young matron has started her new career teaching at Rutgers itself. She is concentrating on trigonometry and calculus and enjoys this more than the high school teaching she did sixteen years ago. Another, with only one semester of retraining, was able to take on modern math instruction of the seventh, eighth and ninth grades when an emergency required her services.

Specialized Education

Not all careers demand a full college degree. There are many jobs available which require only a few months or a few years of training for full preparation. Before spending both time and money on courses, however, it is wise to investigate whether the job you desire is available in your neighborhood. If you decide that you want to be a TV actress, for example, and the majority of programs are filmed far from your home, what's the point? It might be fun to see yourself "on the air" but you can usually find other entertainment as amusing and at lower cost. Secondly, if you decide upon a particular career and the education is not available in the vicinity, think carefully before embarking on a project that will result in an expensive commuting problem. Investigation will prove, we are certain, that you can find both the career and the education necessary for it within both your financial and traveling means. If there is difficulty in either direction, we do suggest that you examine your second choice. It may be the more prudent one.

The three main sources of adult education (excluding the college programs discussed on the preceding pages) include the adult education courses offered by local Boards of Education, the specialized private schools and the correspondence and home study courses.

Adult Education

If you live in a fairly large city, chances are there will be a number of sources of adult education. Because each state controls its own education, the number of courses given varies from state to state, but in most cases, the state does try to meet the needs of the community. Usually these courses are given in the evening at the local high schools and are free of charge. More information on such courses can be had by consulting with the Education Offices in your state. See list following:

STATE EDUCATION OFFICES

State and City	State Director of Vocational Education	State Employment Service Director
Alabama, Montgomery	State Department of Education	State Office Bldg.
Alaska, Juneau	P.O. Box 1841	P.O. Box 2661
Arizona, Phoenix	400 Arizona State Bldg.	1720 West Madison St.
Arkansas, Little Rock	State Education Bldg.	P.O. Box 2981
California, Sacramento	721 Capital Ave.	800 Capital Ave.
Colorado, Denver	State Office Bldg.	1210 Sherman St.
Connecticut, Hartford	P.O. Box 2219	92 Farmington Ave.
Delaware: Dover	313 South State St.	
Wilmington		601 Shipley St.
Dist. of Columbia	Franklin Adm. Bldg.	1724 F St. NW
Florida, Tallahassee	Capitol Bldg.	Caldwell Bldg.
Georgia, Atlanta	State Office Bldg.	State Labor Bldg.

BACK TO SCHOOL

Hawaii,		
Honolulu	P.O. Box 2360	P.O. Box 3680
Idaho,		
Boise	610 Main St.	P.O. Box 520
Illinois:		
Springfield	415 Centennial Bldg.	
Chicago		165 North Canal St.
Indiana,		
Indianapolis	215 State House	10 North Senate St.
Iowa,		
Des Moines	State Office Bldg.	112 Eleventh St.
Kansas,		
Topeka	State Office Bldg.	401 Topeka Blvd.
Kentucky,	State Department of	
Frankfort	Education	Capitol Office Bldg.
Louisiana,	State Department of	
Baton Rouge	Education	P.O. Box 4094
Maine,	State Department of	
Augusta	Education	331 Water St.
Maryland,		
Baltimore	301 West Preston St.	1100 North Eutaw St.
Massachusetts,		
Boston	200 Newbury St.	881 Commonwealth Ave.
Michigan,		
Lansing	P.O. Box 928	
Detroit		7310 Woodward Ave.
Minnesota,		
St. Paul	658 Cedar St.	369 Cedar St.
Mississippi,		
Jackson	P.O. Box 771	P.O. Box 1699
Missouri,	State Department of	
Jefferson City	Education	421 East Dunklin St.
Montana,		
Helena	State Capitol	P.O. Box 1728
Nebraska,		
Lincoln	State Capitol	P.O. Box 1033
Nevada,	State Department of	
Carson City	Education	P.O. Box 602
New Hampshire,		
Concord	State House Annex	34 South Main St.
New Jersey,		
Trenton	175 West State St.	28 West State St.

New Mexico, Santa Fe	State Department of Education	
Albuquerque		P.O. Box 1799
New York: Albany	State Department of Education	
New York		500 Eighth Ave.
North Carolina, Raleigh	State Department of Education	P.O. Box 589
North Dakota, Bismarck	State Department of Education	P.O. Box 568
Ohio, Columbus	220 S. Parsons Ave.	427 Cleveland Ave.
Oklahoma: Stillwater	1515 West 6th Ave.	
Oklahoma City		American National Bldg.
Oregon, Salem	105 State Lib. Bldg.	513 Public Service Bldg.
Pennsylvania, Harrisburg	P.O. Box 911	Seventh and Forster Sts.
Rhode Island, Providence	Roger Williams Bldg.	24 Mason St.
South Carolina, Columbia	State Department of Education	P.O. Box 995
South Dakota: Pierre	State Department of Education	
Aberdeen		310 Lincoln St.
Tennessee, Nashville	Cordell Hull State Office Bldg.	Cordell Hull State Office Bldg.
Texas, Austin	Texas Education Agency	TEC Bldg.
Utah, Salt Lake City	State Department of Education	P.O. Box 2100
Vermont, Montpelier	State Office Bldg.	P.O. Box 435
Virginia, Richmond	State Department of Education	Broad-Grace Arcade
Washington, Olympia	P.O. Box 250	P.O. Box 367

BACK TO SCHOOL

West Virginia, Charleston	State Department of Education	State Office Bldg.
Wisconsin, Madison	14 North Carroll St.	105 South Blair St.
Wyoming: Cheyenne Casper	State Department of Education	P.O. Box 760

We recently had the experience of interviewing two far-sighted women who decided to take advantage of the stenography and typing offered by their local high schools. When Mrs. F. and Mrs. I. each completed the one-year course, they could rival, in a mature way, of course, the Katharine Gibbs' graduates. These two women began thinking vaguely of "doing something" about the time their teenage daughters were juniors in high school. Since Mrs. F. had worked as a file clerk before she married, she had some idea of office procedure. She also remembered the frustration at that time of trying to get a better job without shorthand and typing skills. Determined not to fall into the same trap again, she checked into the various schools and colleges that were offering courses in secretarial skills. She found that the courses offered by the Board of Education were as good as any offered in her vicinity. She outlined her plan of study to Mrs. I. who promptly became her partner, and together they attacked shorthand, typing, bookkeeping, business English, commercial correspondence, and office procedure. Like their daughters, they spent their spare time doing homework, but the result was a smooth sail from kitchen to career.

Community Services Schools

Very often the exact course you have in mind will be given by one of the community services in your vicinity.

The YWCA (Young Women's Christian Association) and the YWHA (Young Women's Hebrew Association) have extensive adult education programs in many of the large cities. Also check with your local branch of the American Association of University Women for their study programs.

Private Vocational Schools

Look at the yellow pages in your phone book and gasp at the number of private schools that are available to you. Naturally the number of schools varies with the size of the city and employment opportunities available in that specific locale. Generally, if jobs are available, schools will also be available. We must warn you to use caution in looking for a special school or course. There are some schools that capitalize on the "glamour industries," promising thousands of job openings and free placement when the individual has completed the instruction. Often these schools do not fulfill their promises, and while the individual is taught a specific vocation, there is little or no demand for the skill. Schools may conjure up visions of successful placement, even citing several case histories; but if there is a limited market, chances are that it will be difficult for a "mature beginner" to get a job in the field.

If a job is really your end in attending school, then do be practical. Just as radio announcing is probably for the lucky few, stenography, typing and bookkeeping are for the fortunate thousands. Other educational areas that might be fun but probably impractical are foreign languages, modern dance, musicology, art, history—any of the more esoteric fields. Mind you, we are not condemning these subjects—we are only being pragmatic, and in the achievement of ends, some graces must be put aside.

Those courses or schools that will aid you in your ultimate search for a job will probably be in the fields of accounting, beauty culture, business, business machines, bookkeeping, telephone boards, hotel management, medicine and dentistry, designing, dietetics, drafting, dressmaking, electrolysis, insurance, real estate, and interior decorating, to name but a few. All of the job opportunities we have listed in this book are backed by courses in either high schools, vocational schools (both public and private), correspondence schools, community colleges and community services, or colleges and universities.

Community Colleges

Not quite colleges, but more than vocational schools, the community colleges are now serving as stepping-stones to college or to a career. A community college has a full two year program, the completion of which will entitle the student to an Associate of Arts Degree. This degree can then be used in obtaining positions—depending upon the educational requirements of the job—or be used as the first two years of a fully-accredited college. There are now close to seven hundred community colleges throughout the country. Many of these colleges are state- or city-supported. The number of courses of study offered varies with each school, but the schools are usually highly regarded, and we strongly suggest investigation before selecting a school. Admission requirements are far more flexible than for the standard four-year college, and some community colleges admit worthy adults who are not high school graduates but who can demonstrate ability to handle college level study.

Correspondence Schools

The correspondence school may be the answer if you live in an isolated area, or if you are tied to the house because of family responsibilities. Provided you have the discipline and aptitude for home study, the number of courses offered through correspondence schools is generous and can lead to the desired degree.

The National Home Study Council, a voluntary organization of accredited home study schools, stated in 1960 that about 1½ million students (about 25 percent of all students) were enrolled in private home study schools. Add to this the number of students enrolled in university extension correspondence courses and government-sponsored courses, and the figure climbs to almost 2,000,000.

The range offered by vocational home study courses includes; advertising, arts and crafts, bookkeeping, computer programming, dressmaking and design, fashion design and illustration, filing, furniture upholstery, interior decoration, jewelry making, secretarial, medical secretarial, photography, real estate, salesmanship, shorthand, steno-typing, accounting, child care, clerical skills, cost accounting, data processing, dental assistance, drafting, economics, home economics, hotel management, law (business, hotel and professional), hotel operation, photo coloring, record keeping, restaurant management, retail buying, showcard and sign lettering, business statistics, technical writing.

Large as the above list is, it is by no means complete.

It does, however, represent the basic courses which, upon completion, will serve to enhance the mature student's vocational skills. Courses in French, Spanish, creative writing, script writing, floral arrangements, etc., may be fun and add zest to your life, but, alas, do not translate into a job future.

To get a complete directory of accredited private home study schools, simply send a postal card to the National Home Study Council, 2000 K Street, N.W., Washington 6, D.C.

Television Courses

There is a *National Compendium of Televised Education* that lists all the televised educational facilities in the country. This Compendium is the only comprehensive reference of its kind, and we suggest that, if you are interested in continuing your education through this method, you write to Michigan State University, Continuing Education Service, University of the Air, Kellogg Center, Room 14, East Lansing, Michigan. The cost of the most recent publication is $4.00.

Costs of Education

Money invested wisely multiplies rapidly. And money invested in educating yourself, if wisely managed, can only lead to financial gain. We cannot stress enough how tremendous an asset education is for the job seeker. A skill is a passport to success. In every field, the more highly skilled person gets the higher wage. In "white-collar-work" the typist receives a higher salary than the clerk, the stenographer, higher than the typist, the secretary, higher than the stenographer, and on and on. Should a woman be fortunate enough to land a highly paid clerical job without any skill, it is the exception rather than the rule.

When you consider the cost of tuition, you should also consider the number of years that you intend to work. Amortize tuition costs over three years, and you will discover that you are paying a low price indeed for what you hope to gain.

The costs of schools range from location to location. It is simple to check whether a school is offering a legitimate course at a legitimate price. All you need do is call your local Better Business Bureau for confirmation. Many schools offer free placement after completion of the required course of study, and when choosing a school, this is an important point to consider.

PART THREE

CHAPTER VI | *Never Too Late For A Profession*

In this section we shall consider those jobs which do not pertain to the government but which, nevertheless, require a bachelor's degree and, in some cases, graduate work. Some of the categories will, of course, be the same as described in the later government chapter. It is wise to bear in mind constantly that the chances of securing full-time employment as a "trainee" in a particular field may vary from state to state. Before launching yourself on long and expensive preparation for a career in any one of these fields, be sure to make a study of whether such jobs will be open to you upon completion of your education. All of the associations officially representing the following professions stated that there would be a willingness to accept the mature woman returning to work. The rest is up to you.

Architecture

A career in architecture can be an exciting adventure. In the words of the American Institute of Architects, "The architect weds functions, the planning and relationship of spaces to meet human needs, to structure, the method of enclosing a space, and to beauty, that quality of art without which no building can qualify as architecture." It is forecast that, since the population growth in the United States will double by the year 2000, and 80 percent of this growth will take place in urban areas, the field of architecture will grow apace. Within the field there are six large areas of professional services that are necessary. Again we quote the American Institute of Architects:

> *Project Analysis Services*—Feasibility studies, financial analysis, location and site analysis, operational programming, and building programming.
> *Promotional Services*—Land Assembly, project financing, promotional design and planning, public relations, and communications.
> *Design and Planning Services*—The normal work of the architect as discussed above under Program, Design Drawings and Construction Documents, with additional emphasis upon maintenance planning and project cost analysis.
> *Construction Services*—The normal work of the architect as discussed above under Contract Administration, with additional emphasis upon job-cost accounting and construction management.
> *Supporting Services*—Those services of engineering, urban planning, landscape architecture, interiors, etc., that have always been a part of architectural practice, and that in recent years have developed into full-time disciplines.
> *Related Services*—Educational and industrial consultation, research and testing, project design, graphics, and prefabrication processes.

To be an architect, the individual must have certain basic aptitudes. She should be able to draw and sketch well enough to present a concept in visual terms. She should have a good eye for the size and shape of volumes and spaces. Any housewife who has carefully selected furniture for her apartment, enlarged rooms or built additions to houses will understand the need for dimension perception. She should be good at the basic skills of mathematics and not afraid to tackle some of the higher mathematical problems. She must be able to synthesize ideas, persevere and be able to work under pressure. And she must be ready to spend a lot of time on her job. At the present writing, there are almost thirty thousand registered architects in the United States. Salaries for beginning architects range from five to six thousand per annum; for experienced, between twelve and fifteen thousand. Jobs are found mainly in the metropolitan areas and in those cities along the south-east, western and eastern seaboards.

For more information on accredited schools of architecture, job opportunities and other pertinent materials, write to the Directors, Professional Programs, American Institute of Architects, 1735 New York Ave., N.W., Washington 6, D.C. A book that may interest you is:

Architect, Creating Man's Environment, Robert W. McLaughlin, The Macmillan Co., New York City, 1962.

Dietetics and Nutrition

Traditionally, a woman's place is in the home, and much of the home activity centers around the kitchen. What could be more natural therefore than to apply your culinary talents, knowledge and planning to a professional career? Not only do these talents help in the preparation for a career in dietetics, but your added years can be an advantage rather than a detriment. A recent survey made by the American Dietetic Association revealed that more than half of its membership was within the age range of thirty-six to sixty-plus. Although about half of this number were not employed at the time of the survey, 64.2 percent did indicate that they intended to return to work within the next six years. And the average age of those who had sought reinstatement in recent years was 45.5 years. It appears evident that dietetics is a field that welcomes the mature woman.

Professional dietetics, although around forty years old, reaches back into antiquity. About a thousand years before Hippocrates, the writings of a gentleman in the Ebers papyrus contained what is probably the first recorded diet prescription. Hippocrates, too, felt that disease could be treated through the proper use of diet. The notorious Roman epicure Apicius gave the world its first cookbook. And so it goes. With each recorded step in history, man has recorded his advances into techniques of diet and nutrition. As the knowledge of dietetics has grown, the branches of service have widened. It is now possible to specialize in hospital dietetics, nutrition programs, commercial food service, school and college food service, scientific research, and teaching and writing.

Dietetics is a job that will probably not be automated. It is a job that is essentially human and requires a great deal of human interaction as well as professional skill. The demand for qualified and specialized personnel is growing in direct proportion to our growth in population. For example, a hospital dietitian may specialize in any one of the following areas: *administrative dietetics*—where she manages, employs, purchases, plans and instructs; *therapeutic*—where she combines managerial and scientific education to plan the diets for patients; *clinic*—where she is involved in instructing patients who are not hospitalized in the proper use of diet; *teaching*—where she works with students and instructs them in all phases of dietetics. In a small hospital, the dietitian may be in charge of all nutrition services. In a small community of towns, one dietitian may devote a few days to several hospitals, supervising and training personnel to fulfill dietary functions. (See also chapter on government.)

Colleges and universities also afford opportunity for dietitians. In most cases, the qualifications are similar to those for a hospital dietitian, the main difference being that the school dietitian is feeding healthy young people.

Many elementary and secondary schools have school lunch programs which a woman may be able to conduct without proper credentials. We know of one lady in a small eastern township who began as a kitchen helper on a part-time basis in the same school her nine-year-old daughter attended. The child complained bitterly about the tastelessness of the food, and her mother began making mild suggestions to the cook. When her ideas were adopted, the difference in food consumption was immediately apparent. The children ate and asked for seconds. Through the years that followed (her daughter is now a sophomore in college), the mother began to take over more and more of the planning, administrating, and developing of the school lunch program. She used her summers for special seminars, and studies on her own. Because of the extraordinary ability she demonstrated, she was given full charge of two of the schools, even though she did not have a high school diploma. This kind of success story is unusual, we know, but indicative of how open the field really is. Obviously, we do suggest special training, but a will can certainly pave a way in this field, as in many others.

Business organizations, commercial food services, and industrial food services offer increasingly more opportunity to the dietitian. As the size of organizations grows, and the installation of company cafeterias becomes the dominant trend, the jobs become more plentiful. A good knowledge of arithmetic is a boon in dietetics, for inventory keeping, planning and balancing are musts. A flair for writing combined with a scientific background might be put to good use since the various media including magazines, newspaper, radio and television are always interested in news that has to do with diet and nutrition.

If you do not have a degree, it is best to look into the back-to-school programs and begin planning early for a dietitian's career. To be qualified (ADA membership), it is also necessary to take a year of internship in a hospital or institution. If you already have a liberal arts degree, it would be wise to write to the American Dietetic Association, 620 N. Michigan Avenue, Chicago, Illinois, for information on recommended courses for qualification. The Association will send you a list of qualified schools and universities. As we have already stated, opportunities appear to be good; starting salaries at present are in the five thousand per annum range, and experienced dietitians can hope to earn in the neighborhood of seventeen thousand. Read *Dietetics As A Profession* and *Dietitians in Demand* for more background material.

There is also a move afoot to make more part-time

jobs available in the field. It is the opinion of the ADA that the number of qualified dietitians who are not working stems directly from the pressure of home duties. If more part-time jobs become available, it will be easier to learn the profession while continuing with one's own responsibilities.

Educational Professions—
Nursery, Elementary, Secondary

Teaching is perhaps the most significant career open to the mature woman. Job opportunities exist in all parts of the country. Most schools and colleges are desperately attempting to fill classroom gaps that threaten to retard the progress of education. Because of this shortage, the colleges, the community and the incumbent teaching staffs are all cooperating to make the teaching road a more tractable one. Since the first bumper crop of post-war babies, educators have been seriously concerned about providing enough schools and teachers to keep in step with America's educational needs.

Back in 1955, a number of colleges were already cooperating with several communities. Stop-gap measures such as emergency licenses and accelerated courses were put into effect. Courses and programs were designed to meet maximum requirements in the minimum amount of time. In general, those women who completed the educational requirements and who spent some time teaching found that working with children, helping them to learn, and being involved in their academic progress socially and in personality adjustment made for a far deeper contribution and personal satisfaction than working in a business office. To quote from a statement by the University of Rochester: "About twenty-five married women, mostly between 35 and 45, were enrolled for two years in an after-school, 2-semester program which earned the six credits required for paid teaching on an emergency certificate. Forty women completed the program and were in great demand as teachers. . . . All the information we have received suggests that they have become successful teachers. We feel that the emergency program attracted mature and able women who made excellent teachers."

The pleasure and gratification experienced by the women who participated in these programs might be summed up by one matron who said, "I haven't had such a good time in fifteen years. All the experiences one has had contribute toward learning to be a teacher. I would like to convince more women who are young and vigorous to go into teaching. It would solve their needs for constructive activity and greater family income and the needs of the schools, too." Even a woman of fifty-five, who retired from business, was able to qualify as a teacher in a rural school.

Teaching is a career highly recommended not only for college graduates who want to return to work, but for women with some college who want to go back to school and then to work. A long list—too long for inclusion here—of the schools that are participating in a special program for teacher training is available from the Women's Bureau of the Department of Labor in Washington, D.C. If the college in your vicinity is not listed, investigate it anyway. It may have joined the program after the writing of this book, or it may be able to help you with a course of study that will fulfill your needs. Other information may also be obtained

NEVER TOO LATE FOR A PROFESSION

from Mrs. Alice K. Leopold, Director, Women's Bureau, U. S. Department of Labor, Washington 25, D.C.

Home Economics

Home Economics has been called the profession with 1,000 job titles. The home economist is found in education, research, business, extension, health, welfare and other important positions. Basically, the major areas break down into teaching and research, business, extension service, institutional, administration and other community service.

Some 45,000 home economists are teaching all levels from elementary to adult education. In addition, many colleges and universities as well as government agencies and private businesses conduct research programs that employ home economists.

In business and industry, we find about 3,500 home economists. Their jobs vary from textile technicians and product testers to information disseminators through the various media of newspapers, magazines, radio and television. The home economist is often the person who bridges the gap between the producer and the consumer.

An additional 5,000 home economists are found in extension services, holding down important county and state positions affecting rural and urban life. The home economist may also go into the dietary services (see preceding section on dietetics) or into community services which serve, for example, as advisers and consultants in public health and welfare agencies.

More than half the home economics work force is over forty, comparing favorably to today's typical woman worker, whose average age is forty.

A college degree is essential. Since there is such a variety of opportunities available, we suggest that you contact the college nearest you to get more information on the home economics courses offered. Write to the American Home Economics Association, 1600 20th Street, N.W., Washington, D.C., 20009. Some correspondence schools also offer courses. Among these schools are:

The National School of Home Study
230 Park Ave., South, New York 3, N.Y.

The American School
Drexel Ave. at 58th St., Chicago 37, Ill.

La Salle Extension University
417 S. Dearborn St., Chicago, Ill.

The International Correspondence Schools
Scranton 15, Pa.

Salaries range from $4,000 per annum for beginners to over $15,000 for the fully experienced. Job opportunities are from good to excellent. For more information, write to the Association for its reading list. Books recommended are *Home Economics as a Profession* by Mildred Thurow Tate (McGraw-Hill); *Home Economics Careers for You* by Velma Phillips, 2nd edition, (Harper & Row). Also, the Home Economics Branch of the U. S. Office of Education, Department of Health, Education and Welfare, Washington 25, D.C., can furnish additional materials.

Library Science

It requires about one year of graduate study to become a librarian. For a liberal arts graduate, this additional study may well be worth the time expended. There are an estimated 64,000 librarians employed throughout the country at the present time. Of these, about 45 percent are employed in school libraries, 30 percent in public libraries and nearly 15 percent in colleges and universities. The remainder are in special libraries and government agencies. By 1970 it is expected that 80,000 trained librarians will be needed. The shortage is such now that graduates get as many as forty job offers. Because the need for librarians is increasing at such a rapid pace, more and more part-time positions will also become available. Many libraries have in-training programs which enable the trainee to get on-the-job experience while he learns.

Library positions are varied and interesting. For example: An order librarian does the purchasing; a cataloguer classifies and catalogues books; a reference librarian helps the public to search out reference materials; a children's librarian plans and directs the children's section; an adult services librarian may help to plan and conduct educational programs on public affairs, art, human relations and other subjects of importance to the community; a young adult services librarian helps to guide young people in the use of library materials; a bookmobile library transports culture throughout rural communities; a school librarian manages the school library, while the college and university librarians run the complex systems of higher learning. Special librarians may be found in small libraries of all types of trade and service organizations, museums, government agencies, research laboratories and other groups.

Salaries start at about $4,800 to $6,000, depending

upon the type of degree, and go to $15,000 for the fully experienced. The general salary scale is similar to that of the teacher.

For more information, read *Library Careers* by Irene and Richard Logodon. Write to: American Library Association, 50 E. Huron, Chicago, Ill.; Special Libraries Association, 31 East 10th St., New York, N.Y.; and the U. S. Office of Education, Library Education Specialist, 400 Maryland Ave., Washington, D.C. And remember to investigate your local library, major business organizations and schools to determine for yourself those positions that might be available.

Law

Be prepared for hard work here. The field is opening to women returning to work, but the number of openings is limited. Once you earn your LL.B.—this is an absolute requirement to practice—any number of positions will be available to you. Almost every industry, social service organization, and small business now employs the services of a lawyer. You can count on from $5000 to $8000 as a starting salary. The sky's the limit, however, for the very experienced. Write to: American Bar Association, 1140 North Dearborn, Chicago, Illinois, for more information.

Mathematics

There are probably more potential mathematicians than one can shake an arithmometer at. The problem is to pry these figure geniuses loose from the drainboard and set them down on the calculus and algebra route. We know of one sixty-year-old grandmother who joined a back-to-school movement and discovered that although she loved the humanities, her real interest lay in figures. She whizzed through high school geometry and algebra, sank her teeth into college mathematics, and at present is well on her way to becoming a mathematics wizard. Unfortunately, at sixty, she will be able to do little more with her skill than teach her grandchildren, but she is getting more enjoyment out of it than she would from a battery of bridge clubs.

Mathematicians are sorely needed in today's scientific economy. A degree in math plus a year of graduate work is desirable. Most of the colleges offer excellent courses in mathematics. Although you will probably be able to do a great deal of work through an accredited correspondence school, we do suggest here that you get your degree from a regular college or university. Most available job openings are to be found in the large cities in the west, north-east and eastern seaboard. Further information can be obtained from the National Science Foundation, 1751 Constitution Ave., Washington 25, D.C.; The U. S. Office of Information, 1776 Pennsylvania Ave., Washington, D.C.; The National Council of Teachers of Mathematics, 1201 16th St., N.W., Washington, D.C.; The Society for Industrial and Applied Mathematics, P. O. Box 7541, Philadelphia 1, Pa.; and The Mathematical Association of America, c/o SUNY, University of Buffalo, 3435 Main St., Buffalo, N.Y., 14214.

Medical/Scientific

Long and arduous training, but well worth it. For those few women who will realize a medical career, the gratification is endless. Only those women with a high scholastic aptitude will be able to make the grade, however, and we suggest that you do some rigid self-testing to determine if you have the interest and dedication. Becoming a doctor of medicine may be too big a program, but if your heart is set on the medical profession, why not look into osteopathy, a system of therapy in which diseases are treated by manipulation of the bones.

Medical Technology

The medical technologists could double in number and still find enough work to go around. This field has been growing steadily since World War II. It now presents some of the most important contributions to human welfare that society has to offer. The medical technologist is the good right arm of a doctor while he is tracking down clues to make a diagnosis. Through the study of body tissues and fluids, the technologist can provide the pathologist with vital information. A qualified technologist should be able to perform several hundred different tests. Through the skill and patience of the technologist, many lives are saved, many diseases cured. From what we have been able to gather, there is no prejudice about hiring a back-to-work woman, provided she has the qualifications.

Requirements for medical technology are not difficult to meet provided you have a scientific bent. Three years of college are necessary before admission is granted to an accredited school. The vital courses consist of sixteen hours of chemistry, sixteen hours of biologic sciences, and one semester of mathematics. The remaining credits can be made up in electives. The next step is to complete the twelve months of instruction in all phases of medical technology in a school of medical technology which is approved by the Council on Medical Education and Hospitals of the American Medical Association. For further information on approved schools in your vicinity, write to: The Registry of Medical Technologists, P.O. Box 44, Muncie, Ind.

An equally important but somewhat less involved profession is that of cytotechnology. This field requires only two years of college, and it deals with cancer detection. The specialist is trained to look for deviant cells that may prove to be cancer cells.

The cost of an education in medical technology may very well be aided by grants and scholarships. The twelve-month training period is usually free of charge or with only minimal covering costs. Starting salaries—from $3600 to $4600 a year in hospitals. Government positions may pay as high as $7500. In some of the larger cities, clinics, especially private clinics, may pay substantially higher than hospitals. Chances for advancement are excellent and employment is year-round. The field is apparently dominated by the fair sex. A whopping 90 percent of the workers are women!

Occupational Therapists

This is a "people" profession. It involves the treatment of a patient through individual or group participation in rehabilitative activity. The people who are treated may have been disabled through accidents or disease; they may be physically or mentally ill; handicapped by birth defects; or they may be senile. Treatment is varied and specialized, including creative manual arts; recreational, educational and social activities; personal care and homemaking; and vocational training. An occupational therapist helps a child to learn to use a paralyzed hand or an older person to relearn the use of arthritic fingers. She works with patients who have lost arms and legs and helps them to train for useful jobs in industry. She is a person who has a smattering of information about many fields, an ingenuity and genuine warmth for people. She wants to help!

Because the shortage of occupational therapists is so great (the number registered in 1963 was about 7,000, and it is projected that by 1966 some 15,000 will be needed) there are many organizations willing to underwrite the educational costs. If you already have your college degree, you may need only an additional eighteen or twenty-two month course leading to a certificate or diploma of proficiency. Majors in biology, psychology, sociology, physical education, home economics and art usually have covered the prerequisites. If you are going back to college, be sure to check with your school to determine if the prescribed courses that are given will lead to a B.A. in occupational therapy. For more information and for facts on financial help available, write to: American Occupational Therapy Association, 250 W. 57 St., New York 19, N.Y.

Salaries for occupational therapists compare favorably with those of teachers and health professionals in the community starting at about $5,000 and climbing as high as $10,000.

Optometry

Optometry is an excellent profession for the woman who can afford to spend as many as five years in college and may want to open her own business. Women are acceptable as optometrists, but the number of jobs available in industry, clinics and hospitals is not extensive. The beauty of learning a profession such as optometry is that it can be put to practice in any town, village or city, provided you have the capital to set up shop. The work is interesting. Your hours can be scheduled according to your own needs, and business is generally good. The New York State Optometric Association states that $12,000 is the approximate yearly salary that can be expected once a practice has been established. Before launching on this career, however, do some reading. Recommended books and monographs are: *Education for the Professions*, U. S. Department of Health, Education and Welfare, Office of Education, Washington 25, D.C.; *Your Eyes and Optometry*, The American Optometric Association, Inc., 4030 Chouteau Ave., St. Louis 10, Mo.; *Occupational Brief, No. 34*, Science Research Associates, 57 West Grand Ave., Chicago 10, Ill.; *Planning Your Professional Career, Optometry*, by The American Optometric Association, 4030 Chouteau Ave., St. Louis 10, Mo.; *Your Opportunity as a Lady O.D.*, by The American Optometric Association, 4030 Chouteau Ave., St. Louis 10, Missouri. Also, the New York State Optometric Association, 250 W. 57 St., New York 19, N.Y., will be able to give valuable information.

Osteopathy

This form of practice is gaining respect in the medical world. The training period comprises four full years of study at a college of osteopathy plus one year of internship. However, you may be admitted into a college of osteopathy with only ninety undergraduate credits, if these credits cover the basic entrance requirements. If you haven't completed your undergraduate degree, and now have the time to spend in college, osteopathy may be the answer.

Women now number only seven percent of all the osteopathic physicians in practice. But we are assured by the American Osteopathic Association that there is no discrimination as to salary or prestige positions. Actually women are regarded as especially suited to such specialties as obstetrics, gynecology and pediatrics.

For more information, write to the American Osteopathic Association, 212 E. Ohio St., Chicago 11, Ill. Literature available in the field includes: *Career in Osteopathy* by Royce E. Brewster, *Guidance Leaflet No. 23*, U. S. Office of Education, Washington, D.C.; "Educational Supplement," reprint, published annually in the January issue of the *Journal of the American Osteopathic Association; The Osteopathic Profession*, Division of Public and Professional Service, American Osteopathic Association, 1960; "Abstract of Laws Governing the Practice of Osteopathy," *Booklet #13; Osteopathy as a Career*, The Institute of Research, 537 S. Dearborn St., Chicago, Ill.; *The Osteopathic Physician and Surgeon*, by Wilfrid E. Belleau, Park Publishing Company, 4141 W. Vliet St., Milwaukee, Wisconsin, and *Opportunities in Osteopathy* by Lawrence W. Mills, Vocational Guidance Manuals, Inc., 20-22 48th Avenue, Bayside 61, N.Y.

Orthoptics

Orthoptics is an allied field of optometry, but one that does not require the investment in training and capital. It is a growing field that appears to be ideally suited to women, since it primarily involves working with children who are cross-eyed. Basically, orthoptics is the science of helping children to see straight. At present, the requirement for an orthoptic technician is two years of college plus technical training which may be received from a certified technician. Generally, starting salaries are about four hundred dollars a month. For more information get in touch with The American Orthoptic Council, 4200 N. Woodward Avenue, Royal Oak, Michigan. Also contact the opthalmological clinics in your vicinity to see if this work is being done.

Physical Therapist

The physical therapist looks at life vigorously and courageously and conveys this outlook to her patients. Essentially, physical therapy is the treatment of patients with disabilities that have resulted from disease or injury. The treatments consist of the scientific use of exercise, heat, cold, water, light, electricity, sound, and massage. Through physical therapy the patient may gain relief from pain, relearn to use limbs that were useless, or learn to function on artificial limbs.

There is absolutely no question about the need for more and more physical therapists throughout the world. In this country, many jobs remain unfilled for lack of professional personnel. Maturity in a worker adds to rather than detracts from her qualifications. If one is physically fit there is no age limit. There are several cases of women in their seventies and retired, who came back to work on request because the need was so great. There is also a definite need for part-time workers in hospitals and clinics. Highly favorable working conditions are reserved for the person with the necessary qualifications.

If you are going back to school, it is possible to get a degree in physical therapy in an accredited four-year course for therapists which includes clinical training. Check your local college for further information. If you already have a degree, you are eligible to take your certificate in physical therapy. This course runs from twelve to fifteen months. Since the need for physical therapists is so acute, there are a great many sources for financial help.

Starting salaries vary from $4,000 to $5,000 and go up to $10,000. However, count on rapid promotions. Many key positions calling for leadership and administration remain unfilled; therefore, the future is bright.

More information can be obtained by writing to The American Physical Therapy Association, 1790 Broadway, New York, or to your local Physical Therapy Association. Literature on accredited schools, financial aid, further reading materials and general information will be sent to you free of charge.

Psychology

Psychology careers are growing in number each year. But unlike many of the other fields that we have discussed where one may work professionally with only a bachelor's degree, a trained psychologist must have a master's degree or a doctorate. Before considering psychology in any of the various fields, be sure that you will have the time and stamina to carry out the study. Many organizations do give scholarships to would-be psychologists, so money need not be a problem.

To be a psychologist is to be a seeker after knowledge of human behavior. Psychology should not be confused with psychiatry, which is a medical specialty.

NEVER TOO LATE FOR A PROFESSION

Psychology covers a far wider area of study, with only a small percentage of the psychologists counseling.

Today more than 25,000 psychologists work in colleges, universities, federal, state and municipal governments, industry, private organizations and public and private schools. They study people and animals for knowledge of behavior and motivation. They attempt to apply this knowledge to the betterment of human welfare. For example, the psychologist studies the effects of tranquilizers and space travel on the body, probes behavior patterns of old age and the environmental causes of prejudice, conducts job training and testing, and analyzes learning and teaching methods. Name the human problem, and you probably will find a psychologist sniffing out the reasons for its existence. Although still a young science, psychology is expanding so rapidly into so many problem areas that its growth is impossible to predict.

For the woman who wants to take the time and trouble to become a psychologist, the field is wide open at any age. Many positions are available in private and in governmental agencies. The Veterans Administration has a special university coordinate training program, which assists graduate students to work and go to school at the same time. Starting salaries for the fully qualified are from about eight thousand to eighteen thousand. For more information write to: Executive Secretary, Central Board of U. S. Civil Service Examiners, Veterans Administration, Washington 25, D.C. For information on other fields, write to the American Psychological Association, Inc., 1333 Sixteenth St., N.W., Washington 6, D.C. Books and pamphlets that may be useful number in the hundreds. A few that may give you further insight are: *Training in Clinical Psychology*, by V. E. Raimy, published by Prentice-Hall, 1959; *The Profession of Psychology*, by W. B. Webb, published by Holt, Rinehart & Winston, 1962, and *America's Psychologists* by E. E. Clark, published by the American Psychological Association, 1957.

Social Work

The ever-expanding field of social work grows with the population. At this writing, over 100,000 more people are needed to fill job vacancies. Although some jobs are obtainable with a college bachelor's degree in any subject (these are mainly in city and state welfare departments), the majority of social work positions call for a master's degree from an accredited school of social work. There are more than sixty accredited graduate schools of social work in the United States and Canada. Since the need for social workers is so great, there are numerous scholarship provisions for those interested in this occupational area.

Admission to a school of social work requires a bachelor's degree from an accredited four-year college.

Social work covers a broad field of activity. We have already mentioned the public welfare programs. In addition a social worker may function with a family care unit, work on the placement of children in foster homes, or be a member of a counseling service—helping entire families in trouble. She may assist distressed travelers. She may work in mental hygiene units. She may work in hospitals as a medical social worker. Or she may choose to be a group worker, taking part in after-school programs. Frequently her job requires professional collaboration with teachers, doctors, psychologists, psychiatrists, judges, lawyers, nurses, the clergy and other professional personnel. Often, she is the key figure in holding a family unit together when it is in a state of crisis.

Because her role is so vital, her training must be extensive. A master's degree from a school of social work requires two full years of study, with much of the time spent in field work. It is, however, extremely likely that an interested party will receive a full-two-year scholarship if she shows real intention of entering the field. We know of a woman who at the age of forty-two decided to become a social worker. She found it necessary to go back to undergraduate school to take the necessary courses in sociology and psychology to meet the entrance requirements. Then she applied to several family service agencies for their scholarship program and was immediately accepted. She then launched into a work-study program that carried her through her M.A. requirements right into family counseling. She is now well on her way to an excellent career. If she decides to go further in her education for a doctorate, there is no doubt that she will be able to apply for a fellowship award that will cover all expenses and provide a healthy monthly income. Her chances for getting the award are excellent.

For further information on schools and requirements, write to the Council on Social Work Education, 345 East 46 St., New York 17, N.Y.; the National Association of Social Workers, 2 Park Ave., New York 16, N.Y. National organizations that may be helpful in supplying information are: American National Red Cross, 17th & D St., N.W., Washington 13, D.C.; Boy Scouts of America, New Brunswick, N.J.; Camp Fire Girls,

65 Worth St., New York 13, N.Y.; Girl Scouts of the U.S.A., 850 Third Ave., New York 22, N.Y.; National Board of the YWCA, 610 Lexington Ave., New York 22, N.Y.; National Federation of Settlements and Neighborhood Centers, 226 W. 47 St., New York 36, N.Y.; National Jewish Welfare Board, 145 E. 32 St., New York 16, N.Y.; Young Men's Christian Associations of the U. S. A., National Council, 291 Broadway, New York 7, N.Y.

Recommended general reading is as follows: *Social Work Year Book,* National Association of Social Workers, 2 Park Avenue, New York, N.Y.; *The Field of Social Work,* by Arthur E. Fink, Wilson & Conover, published by Holt, Rinehart & Winston, Inc., 1959; *Introduction to Social Welfare,* by Walter A. Friedlander, published by Prentice-Hall, Inc., 1955; *So You Want to Be a Social Worker,* by Helen Harris Perlman, published by Harper & Brothers, 1962; *Social Work— An Introduction to the Field,* Second Edition, by Herbert H. Stroup, published by American Book Company, 1960.

CHAPTER VII | *Office Life*

There is always an office job to be filled for the woman who wants to go back to work. Industry, from glamorous advertising agencies to prosaic feed grain companies, from giant corporations to humble "1-man" offices, offers tremendous opportunities for the mature job seeker. Because there is a shortage of skilled clerical personnel and a broadening awareness of the value of the mature job seeker, the field of office work offers unlimited possibilities. There is no shortage of job potential. Working conditions are, for the most part, excellent. Most companies are operating on a 37½-hour week schedule, many on a 35-hour week with coffee breaks both in the morning and afternoon. There is almost no Saturday work, and the forty-hour week has gone the way of the hooped skirt. A two-week vacation is now the minimum, plus all of the legal holidays, some religious holidays, and in the larger companies a set policy of sick leave. Many of the non-profit organizations offer up to three and four weeks of vacation after a specified number of years of employment. In most large cities, air-conditioning is the rule, adequate work space a company policy, and new equipment a priority.

To add to the "unseen" benefits of office work, white-collar workers are assured a 12-month job each year. No layoffs! Each year that the individual is employed by the company, she is gaining more security, increased financial return and greater status within the company, as well as, in many cases, sizable amounts of money in profit-sharing. Her time is well invested. It may sound astonishing, but it is nevertheless a fact—office jobs are not only easy to prepare for, but also easy to get! Any woman with common sense and ambition, who is courteous, self-controlled and cooperative, will find it relatively simple to acquire the additional skills necessary to prepare herself to become an office worker. The last U. S. census reports that white-collar occupations absorb 32.4 percent of the employed women in the United States, with an upward trend expected in the '60's and '70's.

In acknowledgment of industry's desperate need, we are now devoting this chapter to an analysis of clerical job requirements. But first it must be borne in mind that not all jobs are open to the mature woman; a good many jobs are indeed available, and it is these jobs that should be made her target. If concentration is placed in the right areas, there will be a bull's-eye every time. The jobs to steer clear of are the so-called "glamour" jobs—the jobs that are the tinsel and decoration of the work world. Where the field is peppered with bright ambitious young men and women, such as in some parts of advertising, television and theatre, the chances of success for the returnee are minimal. Organizations such as publishing, education, social services, government, industry, etc., do welcome the qualified mature woman.

The Secretary

Perhaps the greatest lack in the nation's job economy is of capable women carrying steno pads. Under any name—steno-clerk, stenographer, gal Friday, clerk-typist with steno, administrative assistant, etc.—she still remains that hard-to-find individual who can "take a letter." Stripping away the confusing trappings of job titles, Career Blazers feels that every job requiring stenography has "the shape of secretary" whether it be junior or executive or fall someplace in the vast middle range of secretarial posts. However, a similarity in job title does not mean that each job is also equal in duties, responsibilities, and interest. The variables are too numerous to mention. Take, for example, the editorial secretary. She will spend much of her time dealing with authors, keeping track of manuscripts, and possibly even doing some light proofreading (if her grammar is par excellence) as well as the usual typing and steno duties. The secretary to a busy engineer might find herself knee-deep in technical correspondence, some of a highly secretive and interesting nature. She might be called upon to do minor research, and if her employer is one who has to travel, set up plane and hotel reservations. A medical secretary may seldom make use of her steno pad, but require every ounce of ability to handle people. She will also undoubtedly relieve her employer of the problems of bill-collecting, talking to medical retailers and the intricate handling of his very busy schedule. Further, if we examine the responsibilities of a secretary to an interior decorator, we find that this "right-arm" will be responsible for such a diversity of jobs as investigating the market, keeping track of new materials, billing, contact with customers, etc. What actually is a secretary then? Broadly, we would call her an assistant to her boss—a teammate. She is the one who frees him so that he can run with the ball. She wards off tacklers with his phone, greets his visitors, shields him from minor disturbances, cleaves a way through one-hundred-and-one intangible annoyances so that he can move forward quickly to his goal. The efficiency of a secretary may mean the difference between a man's promotion and his stagnation within a company.

What Are the Qualifications of a Good Secretary?

The most amazing thing about being a good secretary is that almost anyone can be with a little application and practice. Personality ranks high on the scoring card. She must be poised, diplomatic, and willing to work. She must be cooperative, reliable, and calm. She must also be flexible, thorough, and a person of high integrity and good character. She must possess all of these characteristics plus a technical knowledge of typing and stenography. While in some company situations no premium is placed on knowing stenography, it is always preferable to have this much sought-after skill.

Unfortunately, too large a percentage of those women returning to the business world are not proficient in typing and stenography. Many of the women we interview tell us they will gladly go to school at night to brush up on their skills *after* they have landed a job. It seldom works that way—employers demand the skill *before, not after* a person is hired. Enthusiasm and willingness are excellent attributes, but without skills, the chances of getting a job are substantially lowered.

OFFICE LIFE

In the history of Career Blazers, we have never placed a secretary who could not type. However, all is not lost! It is surprisingly simple to master these skills, and the time it will take is directly proportional to the time and effort one puts into it. Every city has many secretarial schools. Most high schools offer evening courses as do, in many cases, local Y's. If there is an office of the National Manpower Commission in your city, consult with it. Even correspondence schools offer appropriate courses.

For the woman who comes back to work via the steno pad, success can be easily attained. The story of Mrs. Margaret J. is inspiring, and not at all unusual. Mrs. J. came to Career Blazers about four years ago. She had recently been widowed and her two daughters were away at college. While, fortunately, her late husband's insurance protected the completion of her children's education, she found she would soon run out of resources for herself. Also, aside from her financial need for a job, Mrs. J. had a strong need to find something to occupy her time. She had spent the past twenty years as a homemaker, but now she found that this vital job no longer existed. She was lonely, despondent, fraught with a feeling of isolation and uselessness. Her desire to get into the work world was both healthy and constructive. However, a plan of action was necessary. The only thing Mrs. J. was sure of was that she wanted to work; she was totally unaware of what kind of job she would enjoy, nor did she have any idea what industry demanded of its clerical workers. After a discussion with one of our interviewers, a plan of action was decided upon.

The interviewer and Mrs. J., after a series of discussions, finally came to the conclusion that although she was attractive and well-dressed, her lack of skills and office experience left Mrs. J. with only a few choices. She might seek a job requiring no skills, such as file clerk, receptionist, or salesgirl, or take a long-range approach and learn skills. If Mrs. J. chose not to learn skills, she would be faced with the prospect of fewer available jobs as either receptionist or clerical worker. As a salesgirl, she would be on her feet all day and probably work a forty-hour week. Although such jobs would certainly put bread on the table, they might fall short of providing the stimulation and involvement that Mrs. J. was seeking as part of her job package. Fortunately, Mrs. J. still had some savings to fall back on, so the secretarial training became the most likely choice.

Some months later, Mrs. J. returned proudly bearing her certificate from a secretarial school. She now could type sixty words per minute and take Gregg shorthand at the rate of one hundred and ten words a minute. Mrs. J. looked ten years younger, and we realized that it had happened again. The addition of knowledge or the acquiring of a usable skill acts like a long drink from the fountain of youth. It lifts the spirits and the morale, buoys up the self-image and coasts the individual along on a tide of self-approval. All these "intangibles" enhance one's marketability. Mrs. J. realized after several interviews that not only could she get *a* job—she could get several!

Her first interview was tedious and frightening. Her impulse was to take the first job offered. It took a great deal of discussion to convince her that she had a *choice,* and that her selection must be based on something more solid than "someone wants me!" She soon began to enjoy meeting prospective employers. She found that by doing a bit of research as to what kind of positions existed, she could be more certain in her final choice of job. She went on a total of six interviews, becoming more and more relaxed as she progressed. Job hunting changed from a terrifying dip in the cold waters of work society to an exhilarating experience of meeting interested and interesting people. From the six interviews she went out on, she reaped three job offers. The first offer was a position with the fund-raising department of an organization involved in assisting retarded children. Here she would be in charge of writing receipts for contributions, handling routine correspondence to volunteer workers, assisting in the arrangement of meetings, fund-raising functions and events, as well as taking minutes at the monthly staff meetings. The second job was in the personnel department of a major blue chip company. A busy job, it entailed keeping voluminous personnel records, taking care of involved chores with hospitalization, insurance and retirement plans, correspondence, heavy telephone contact with executive members of the organization and employment agencies as well as full reception duties. The third offer was the highest-paying. It meant being virtually a busy one-man-office. The nature of the job was to do everything necessary to keep the office running, including simple bookkeeping. Although Mrs. J. had not trained in bookkeeping, she was assured that the system was simple and that the accountant would be pleased to teach her the fundamentals.

Mrs. J. threw the problem into our laps. She simply did not know which job to accept. And although one can never really know a job until one has been on it, it is still possible, through analysis of the jobs offered, to make the wisest choice. The one-man office, it was decided, would be too pressured. Mrs. J. felt too inexperienced to cope with the complete responsibility of managing a small office. She felt that if she were to come down with a cold she would be torn between nursing the cold and covering the office. Another important factor was that Mrs. J. did want to be among people, and the one-man office might increase her sense of loneliness. The additional monies offered on this job did not compensate for the liabilities. Making a choice between the two remaining jobs proved more difficult, however. Both jobs offered the same salary, good locations and stimulating work atmospheres. She liked equally her prospective employers. She toyed with just flipping a coin but decided to sleep on it overnight. In the morning, she called us and told us her decision. It was indeed a wise one. After much soul-searching, she found that despite her success in landing several jobs, she was still not sure of her ability to *keep* a job. Since the position with the non-profit organization did not offer unemployment benefits, she chose the personnel job in the industrial firm. Her fear gave her the clue to her choice, and became the deciding factor. Very happily, she called the firm and told them that she would be pleased to report to work that coming week. Several weeks later we again heard from Mrs. J. but this time in an official capacity. She was listing several jobs with us, and mentioned in passing that her job was progressing magnificently. In time, Mrs. J. became a more responsible member of the firm. She began to screen new applicants and do preliminary interviewing and testing and her progress hasn't stopped yet. We expect her to be made personnel manager on her next promotion!

Mrs. J.'s success could have been predicted. Her enthusiasm and willingness were readily recognized and appreciated. It is an axiom we have seen proven hundreds of times—companies are as eager to find and promote good people as good people are eager to be promoted. Possibly a junior secretary might have been hired instead of Mrs. J., but it is not likely that a junior would have had the maturity and poise that come with the years to merit such quick promotion. Mrs. J. is just one of the many thousands of women we have interviewed who, having decided to return to the business world, has made the transition from homemaker to career girl so gracefully. Of course, not all of these women are in a position to study steno before taking the plunge, but our surveys have shown that those who did were far more successful in terms of job satisfaction and salary promotion.

Sometimes the process of becoming a secretary is more gradual. Mrs. R. was 44 years old when she came to see us. She was distraught and frightened. She had never worked, other than as a volunteer in church organizations and in community projects. Suddenly her husband, who had owned a small but successful hardware business, suffered a major illness which left him incapacitated. He was forced to sell the business and to live a partially sedentary life. Because their expenses were mounting, Mrs. R. could not realistically take the long-range view—she had to find employment immediately. A discussion of her abilities revealed the fact that she was quick with figures, loved adding long columns of numbers, enjoyed detail work and had a clear, legible handwriting. We suggested that she might apply for a job as a figure clerk which would involve posting, checking figures and making bank deposits. Assured that there would be a job for her although at the moment the market was slow, Mrs. R. felt her spirits rally immediately. She realized that even though she was lacking in training, her native abilities were important considerations. Her problem was indeed solvable. Several days later a travel agency called requesting a mature person with a good handwriting and flair for figures. We immediately sent Mrs. R. We were not surprised that she got the job although she was competing with several women who were her juniors. Was it luck that Mrs. R. got the job? We think not. Her sincerity and reliability were evident. Her straightforward approach and honest desire to work came across. It wasn't long before Mrs. R. was promoted to the job of assistant bookkeeper. When her husband's health improved and she had secured a salary increase, she felt she was in a position to make a further decision. Should she study more bookkeeping and aim for a full-charge bookkeeping position or should she study stenography? She decided on the latter because she preferred diversity of duties. A full year later, she returned to see us decked out in a new hat, a new personality and a new assurance. She had now an excellent knowledge of accounts receivable and accounts payable, plus a good working knowledge of stenography and typing. Her rounded office abilities made her a logical candidate for a one-man office. She found such an office near her home, and since her evenings were still occupied with taking care of her husband, the location was ideal. Mrs. R., unlike Mrs. J., preferred the small office, and the higher salary was most attractive.

Specialize or Generalize?

It's never too late to specialize. The secretary who has made the first grade may feel that she wants to go further. There is nothing as motivational as a little success. It is possible to try to reach for the executive secretary level, or to branch into the various secretarial specializations; i.e., legal secretary, medical secretary, or engineering secretary.

Legal Secretary

The legal secretary, as the term implies, works in a law office or the legal department of a major organization. Not only do these jobs demand a familiarity with legal terminology and a respect for the law profession, but also an extremely responsible and meticulous personality. Lawyers actually prefer to hire the more mature person. Generally a legal secretary must be able to take excellent notes, work carefully and quickly on legal documents and meet the lawyer's clients. A secretary who is trained in stenography but wants to move into the legal field will find a number of roads open to her. She can study at night, taking special courses that prepare her for legal work or she can attempt to get a beginning job in the field, and through the gentle process of osmosis, pick up the necessary legal information. On the job, she will begin to learn how to deal with briefs, affidavits, agreements, wills, proxies, powers of attorneys, leases, etc. The more she learns, the greater the dividends; for legal secretarial jobs pay well, afford excellent job security and allow for quick job promotion. As in all secretarial jobs, the legal secretary greets the clients, relieves her employer of a myriad of details, takes charge of his office and even goes to court with him on important cases. Another important feature of legal training is the opportunity for part-time jobs in the larger cities. Many mature women find that they would prefer to work two or three days of the week, rather than full-time. A legal secretary who knows her job can often specify where she will work and what she will be paid.

Court Reporter

The court reporter is probably one of the most highly paid positions open to women in the clerical field. It does, however, require a great deal of practice. Perfection is the key word here. Most reporters use a small machine called the "stenotype." On this machine is produced the verbatim report of a day in court, an annual meeting, an important pro and con session. The information put into the machine is in code, not unlike the shorthand symbols. But the rate of speed can range from 150 to 250 words per minute. The reporter transcribes these notes and presents a finished report in much the same way as a secretary transcribes her notes. Many reporters work on a free-lance basis and earn from $8,000 to $10,000 a year.

Medical Secretary

The medical secretary works for a doctor or in a hospital. To be of top assistance to her employer, she should be familiar with medical terminology. There are many schools and colleges which have special courses to train the medically-minded. There are some medical secretaries who combine the job of medical technician with secretarial skills. A job such as this would require somewhat more prolonged training, but again, the greater the training, the greater the possibility for financial and emotional rewards. On the other hand, there are many doctors' offices where a warm-hearted woman with a moderate amount of skill can ably assist her physician boss.

Dictaphone Secretary

The dictaphone secretary is generally the one who, for some reason, finds it impossible to learn stenography. More and more organizations have recognized the fact that stenography may be a stumbling block and have consequently added some kind of transcribing equipment to their office. The dictaphone is an extremely simple machine to operate. Your employer dictates his material into the machine. His voice is recorded on a tape, a wax roll or a wire, according to the nature of the equipment. The dictaphone secretary takes the recording, listens to the letter once through to get an approximate idea of the length, and then listens again, typing it as she listens. The plus factors of a dictaphone machine are that it will repeat as often as the secretary wishes it to, is completely flexible as to time, and doesn't smoke cigars. But if you like personal contact, better learn stenography after all.

Executive Secretary

The executive secretary is that plum job that the young middle-ager may very well attain. For the office worker with ambition, intelligence and drive, the position of executive secretary is a rewarding position to attain. It is a natural goal for the college woman returning to the job world after a few years of being "re-office broken." But there are some liabilities. Gone are the good old 9-5 days. A real executive secretary is on call days, nights, and week-ends. A combination of witchery, intuition, and fortitude are constantly called upon to solve the hundreds of minor and major crises that arise each day. Your boss may be a man holding an extremely important position, and your job unofficially may be to see that he keeps it. On the rewarding end, the executive secretary enjoys more prestige and respect than any other woman in the company, with the exception of those on the professional staff. Her salary can be as high as or in some cases higher than two hundred a week. Her work is a complex of meeting important visitors from all over the world, highly-placed government officials and royalty, attending vital policy-making meetings, and seeing that her boss's son receives his birthday present.

No woman without office experience can realistically hope to return to the job market and immediately obtain this kind of position, but we have had unusually good success with women who have "returned" and have had some four or five years of recent proven experience behind them.

An "extra" in the applicant's experience can sometimes be the selling point to get her that excellent job. It may be a knowledge of a foreign language, or a proficiency with figures (the executive secretary often is asked to balance her boss's checkbook), or an interesting hobby that will act as the catalyst. We know of one executive secretary who had toyed with interior decorating for many years. After she was on the job several months, the company moved to larger quarters. She suggested that she might be allowed to decorate her boss's suite of offices. He agreed. Not only did she do an outstanding job, but some of the other departments "borrowed" her services.

It goes without saying that top skills, both in shorthand and typing, are an essential for the executive secretary. Her knowledge of grammar, as well, must be perfect. It will also be an asset if she has some acquaintance with world affairs, government, and politics. She must be able to provide both character and business references. And she must look the part—crisp, efficient, and trim.

Personality Plus?

An old cliché, but a true one, when it comes to itemizing the qualities that make a good secretary. At Career Blazers, we've made a close study of the successful executive secretaries and have come up with the following observations. First of all, she considers herself part of an important team, with her boss as head man. She approaches all problems head on, squarely and maturely. She is cooperative, flexible, reliable, honest, has a good sense of humor, likes people and shows it. She knows how to refrain from office gossip and keeps the interests of her company uppermost during her working hours. She is unusually interested in her career (a "must" usually, since she may spend as many as fifty hours a week on her job). She is well-dressed, poised, and diplomatic. The receptionist, the office boy, and the president of the company all like and respect her.

Bound by the Steno Pad? Not Always . . .

We have already mentioned the dictaphone secretarial position, which is in most respects a secretarial job without steno. The gal Friday, that ubiquitous title, is another *nom de plume* for a secretary without steno. The gal Friday may not use the dictaphone, however. She may be asked to compose her own correspondence or copy from hand-written notes that are issued by her boss. Essentially, her duties are the same as those of the secretary. The number of openings varies with the company, although the percentage of well-paying jobs without steno is about 75 percent less than those with steno.

Bookkeeper

Bookkeeping is another important area to consider. Aptitudes with figures can lead to a responsible office position. Figure jobs seem best suited to those women who prefer to work alone. To some women the job of working with figures can be sheer tedium and drudgery; to others, it can be the challenge of seeing that all things come out right in the end. Although a great many bookkeeping procedures can be learned on the job, if one aspires to be a full-charge bookkeeper, it might be best to study in the evenings. Most of the evening high schools give courses in bookkeeping, as do the colleges, correspondence and business schools.

The job of bookkeeper is an extremely important one, and is the one that most often leads to office management. She is the one who pays the bills, issues salary checks, deposits monies, and balances accounts. She is the first to know if the company is losing or making money. Her alertness to the financial situation can often mean a warning in due time to reverse a bad downward business trend. Because of her close proximity to the money matters of the organization, the bookkeeper is at times the confidante of the boss, his right-hand assistant, and if she can take steno, his administrative assistant. Although bookkeeping does not have the glamorous overtones of the executive secretary, it is, nevertheless, an extraordinarily vital position in any organization. The rise to the top can be a quick one as well, since there is as great a shortage in qualified bookkeepers as there is in secretaries.

Clerical Worker

The woman who has neither an aptitude for figures, nor an ability to learn shorthand and typing need not despair! Although the jobs are fewer, there are openings available where an industrious "return-to-worker" can make her weight felt. We recall one woman in her early forties who simply had to work to supplement a small yearly income. We placed her with a firm that made maps, as a map-proofreader. The salary was not high, but the job was quite interesting. Delightedly, she reported back to us the marvel of coming across towns and villages in the United States with names like Intercourse, Dead City, Cherry, Clay, Box Butte, etc. Her sense of humor was so pithy that she made out of what could have been a tedious job an exploration into the wonders of city naming. Six months later, there was a slow period in the organization, and her job was abolished. She came to us again, expectant and eager. Although we were unhappy about her lack of skills, her willingness to take anything heartened us. We next sent her on a file clerk's position with a non-profit organization. The job turned out to be more than a file clerk's menial opening and shutting of drawers. The office turned her loose in a room full of filing cabinets, gave her permission to overhaul the filing system and told her she was on her own. Being of intrepid character, she immediately popped into the library, found some books on the Dewey Decimal System, and proceeded scientifically to revamp the files. Within a short period of time, she was not only promoted but given an assistant. Never in the history of the agency had there been such prompt and efficient filing.

Clerical positions may be found in banks, insurance agencies and industrial companies as well as advertising agencies and book publishers. For that matter, wherever there is an office, there should be several available clerical positions. We work with one publishing company which has offices in a nearby suburb. They tell us they prefer the mature candidate for their clerical positions. They have found that the "returnee" is more eager to work, does a better job and is far more flexible than younger people in that particular area.

Receptionist

Perhaps the most sought-after job by the mature woman is that of receptionist. A tremendous percentage of inexperienced job seekers (both the neophyte and the mature beginner) begin their search by answering ads for receptionists. It is generally assumed that the only qualifications needed for such a position is a ready smile, a pleasing personality, and an ability to handle people. Also, it is generally assumed that here is a job where one can meet people, make friends and perhaps find excitement, adventure, and even romance! Although it is true that these elements do exist, the receptionist's job is, in most cases, a hard-to-get-job, and not necessarily a glamorous one.

The main reason that there is difficulty in landing this job is that, contrary to general belief, skills are very often necessary. A knowledge of one of the telephone boards is also usually required. Even if one has typing, steno and a knowledge of the monitor board, there is still a problem. The number of receptionist jobs in an organization varies with the size of the organization, from one to perhaps ten. The number of secretarial jobs with a company may range from one into the hundreds. Proportionately, there will be many fewer receptionist jobs open each year than secretarial. For every company employing, say, eighty secretaries, two hundred typists, etc., there will still be only one receptionist per floor. As a rule, it is only with large companies that there are positions open for mature receptionists without skills. Although the openings are rare, a woman who has a combination of tact, breeding, personality and a good memory may be lucky enough to land such a position. Several large book publishers and advertising agencies prefer the mature woman returning to work to the young lady who is only using the job as a stepping-stone.

Just recently, one of our junior applicants referred her mother to us. Mrs. M. came to see us, presenting an extremely cultured and refined manner. She held a degree from one of the better women's colleges. Aside from the degree, however, she could offer no skills or office abilities. She had married directly after graduation and had spent the past twenty years raising a family. Mrs. M. really didn't need the money, but she felt she would like to work to relieve the monotony of her long days. As luck would have it, we were called that very morning by one of our clients, a large book publisher, in need of a mature receptionist. We immediately sent Mrs. M. on the interview. She got the job and this time we advised that she accept immediately. She was thrilled to be actually meeting the authors of the books she had been reading. Mrs. M. told us several months later that she felt younger and revitalized by her new career. Each day was a challenging experience. And, of course, the salary gave her unexpected pocket money.

Unfortunately, as we have stated, the incidence of these jobs is small. Usually jobs call for a receptionist in a small office who is asked to do more than meet and greet. She sits at the front desk handling all incoming telephone calls. If the office is very small, she may simply be called upon to run a push-button phone, but usually she is expected to know or have the desire to learn the monitor or switchboard. If she doesn't know the board, she can learn it from the telephone company or a friend who will be good enough to teach her, or attend a business school for a short period of time. At least 75 percent of the receptionist jobs listed also ask for typing. Although typing need not always be fast, it generally must be accurate. Without either the skills of typing or the knowledge of one of the boards, the quest for a receptionist job can be discouraging indeed. If your heart is set on it, do prepare for its requirements.

CHAPTER VIII | *Develop A Technical Skill*

This chapter is primarily for those high school graduates who can afford both the time and money on additional training, but who cannot or do not want to invest in a full four-year college program. There are many interesting and lucrative jobs available that a little direction, a little training and a lot of fortitude will bring within your reach. As you sow, so shall you reap, but before planting your garden, be sure you want the flowers that will come up!

Medicine

Not all medical careers involve years of long training. There are many openings in the field where maturity is an asset, provided that stamina and interest are added to your accumulation of life experience. Some of the careers where there are definite shortages and where training can be had at both minimum expense and time are listed on the following pages.

Dental Assistant

As the job title implies, the function in this job is to assist the dentist. This may include a number of duties ranging from the social (the meeting and greeting of patients) to the development of X-rays, sterilization of instruments, keeping of simple records and billing. Because of the current shortage of trained technicians, dentists have been known to train an intelligent woman in the various duties of their offices. However, we strongly advise that if it is at all possible you take school training rather than rely on the off-chance that such an opening will occur.

Five different training programs for dental assistants are approved by the American Dental Association, including a correspondence course, an evening course, a one-year high school or vocational course, as well as either a one-year or two-year college program. More specific information about these courses can be obtained by writing to the executive secretary, American Dental Association, 410 National Bank Bldg., La Porte, Indiana. This organization will also send you pamphlets and a list of reading materials. Beginners can expect to earn between fifty and seventy-five dollars per week. Salary advancement can go to well over one hundred dollars a week.

Opportunities may be found in your own backyard. Since dentists must practice where many people are congregated, and since a dental practice is often best situated in a specific neighborhood rather than a metropolis, your local dentist may need your help. Openings for either full or part-time help are quite prevalent in this field.

Dental Hygienist

This vocation is perhaps best described as being halfway between the dental assistant and the dentist. The dental hygienist always works under the supervision of a licensed dentist, and is herself an accredited member of the profession. In 1962, approximately ten thousand hygienists were in practice in the United States, and almost all were women. They work in private dental offices, public health agencies or school systems, industrial plants, clinics, hospitals and dental hygiene schools, and as civilian members of the Armed Forces.

Accreditation or licensing is required in almost every state in the Union. Alabama and Georgia are the only states that do not require a license. Since each state has its own examination, a licensed dental hygienist may find it necessary to take additional examinations to practice in other states. Most of the schools provide for a two-year certification course. Some have a four-year program leading to a bachelor's degree. Minimum requirement for admission is graduation from high school, or its equivalent. There are 33 accredited schools of dental hygiene in the country. Scholarships and student loans are available in the field. For other pertinent information dealing with the profession, write to: the American Dental Hygienist Association, 100 East Ohio Street, Chicago 11, Illinois.

The job outlook in dentistry is extremely favorable. Shortages in the field are expected to continue for the next decade. Because of the growing interest in dental care programs for children, this rapidly growing field will need more and more trained technicians. Mature women do extremely well in this occupation for several reasons: there is virtually no competition from men; the youngsters respond well to the mother figure; and work interest is enlivened by the diversity of the job which includes cleaning and polishing the patient's teeth, preparing fillings, developing X-rays, massaging gums, and, of course, much warm, human contact. Salaries are good, ranging from $4,000 for beginners to $10,000 for those with experience.

We know of one woman, slightly over sixty, who has built up a practice solely of cleaning patients' teeth. She has developed an artistry in her profession. Actors and actresses as well as the ordinary you and I find their way to her door because of her unusual interest in maintaining a clean, healthy mouth. She treats each tooth as if it were a jewel—cleaning, buffing and polishing it. Her love of and interest in her work not only pay her handsomely, but give her tremendous job satisfaction and have earned her a name in the professional world.

Nursing

One of the most honored and noble activities in the medical profession is nursing—and it is open primarily to women. Although the concept of nursing evokes in many the image of a dewy-eyed youngster studying hard to become a nurse, the older woman is not only accepted gratefully, but is sought after. If a woman has the stamina and interest in helping other human beings, there is no reason to prevent her from becoming a nurse. One of our favorite stories is about a former trapeze artist who turned to nursing. It seems that her career as a circus performer was abruptly curtailed when she had a near-fatal accident during one of her trapeze acts. Although she did get well and returned to her circus job, she decided that perhaps she should find something to do that would keep both feet

DEVELOP A TECHNICAL SKILL

firmly on ground. Since her hobby had always been to help people when they were sick, she choose practical nursing. Now in her mid-seventies, this remarkable dynamo still carries a full-time job as a nurse at a Florida hospital. She weighs only one hundred twenty-seven pounds, but because she has retained her youthful muscular development can hoist patients almost twice her size in and out of bed. Her interest in and dedication to people are so genuine that she is often actually able to inspire a desire to get well. One young lady, an aspirant of the dance, was stricken with polio and was convinced that she would never dance again. Together, within the hospital's physical therapy program, the young lady and the nurse worked at bringing life back into the crippled limbs. The nurse always had encouraged the patient by saying she would dance again. The young lady did recover mobility in her limbs and today is a dancing teacher.

Nursing is divided into two large areas—practical nursing and registered nursing. Practical nursing does not take as much time to learn, but the practical nurse does not qualify for some of the responsible nursing jobs. It does, however, serve a very necessary function in our society. There are about 225,000 practical nurses employed in the United States. Most of them work in hospitals, clinics, homes for the aged, rest homes, or other institutions where the ill are housed. Almost every state in the Union requires that a practical nurse be licensed, and most states also require that she be a citizen of the United States or have applied for naturalization. Training for a practical nursing vocation generally lasts one year. It can be obtained in vocational schools, vocational high schools, adult education programs, private schools, junior colleges and colleges. Many high schools are beginning to offer courses in practical nursing as a part of their general curriculum. In 1962, there were more than 700 practical nurse training programs and of these, three-fifths were operated by the public school system. Most of the schools require a high school diploma for admission into the programs, but equivalency degrees are generally acceptable. The practical nurse is taught basic nursing skills, body structure and functions, conditions of illness, nutrition and medication. She is also trained in actual nursing situations.

Since there is still a shortage of registered nurses, the employment future looks promising through the sixties. Average weekly earnings range from about forty-five dollars to seventy-five dollars on beginning jobs. Usually the practical nurse earns about three-quarters the pay that a registered nurse receives in a given geographic area. For further information, write to the National Association for Practical Nurse Education and Service, 475 Riverside Drive, New York 10027, and the National Federation of Licensed Practical Nurses, Inc., 250 W. 57 St., New York 10019.

Registered Professional Nurse

A registered professional nurse is the person who has completed all the requirements for state registration. She is one of the key people in the care of the sick, for she is either giving direct care to patients or she is supervising allied nursing personnel. Her job is a complex and responsible one and her value is not to be underestimated. Besides providing care in hospitals,

DEVELOP A TECHNICAL SKILL

the registered nurse also is employed as a private duty nurse in the home, office nurse, public health nurse, occupational health or industrial nurse, and nurse educator. Nurses may also do research, editing and perform special public education functions.

Nurses may be trained in either the diploma, baccalaureate or associate degree programs. The diploma program is usually conducted by hospitals and generally requires three years of experience, the bachelor's degree program of four to five years' training is conducted in a school or university; and the associate degree program which takes approximately two years is conducted by junior and community colleges. All professional nursing programs include a combination of both classroom instruction and supervised nursing practice.

The more mature woman may find that the studying required to become a registered nurse is somewhat more difficult than for a practical nurse. However, the salary remunerations are higher, the general employment picture is somewhat more stable, and the possibility of advancement into jobs such as those for administrators, teachers, clinical specialists and public health nurses is, of course, brighter. Average salary at the current writing seems to be about $100 a week for experienced nurses in hospitals; somewhat lower for those who are just starting out, and slightly higher for nurses in private duty.

For more information, write to the National League for Nursing, Committee on Careers, 10 Columbus Circle, New York 10019, and the American Nurses Association, 10 Columbus Circle, New York 10019.

Other Hospital Jobs

Some hospital jobs for which virtually no training is necessary can be found most readily, such as jobs for orderlies, nurses' aides, hospital attendants and psychiatric assistants. Salaries are relatively low, but often these jobs may be had on either full-time or part-time schedules. For further information, contact your local hospital or health center.

Hotel Occupations

Rapid technological changes, automation and shorter work weeks are producing a new phenomenon in our culture—the growing movement toward more leisure time. People have more time and money to spend, and the industry that stands to benefit most from this new economic development is the hotel and motel industry. In 1962, six hundred thousand men and women were employed in this field, and a large percentage (nearly half) were mature women. A further advantage of a career in this particular industry is its wide distribution over rural, village and city areas. Since Americans have become motorized, motels even in unlikely or thinly populated areas may still do well, provided they are on a main artery. Getting a job in the motel or hotel in your area may be relatively simple. For the untrained, a number of clerical and clean-up jobs will be available. Naturally, these jobs, like all non-skilled jobs, pay relatively little. However, with proper training, work in this industry can become a career.

The "hospitality" business offers a great deal to the mature woman. Because there is such a shortage of trained motel and hotel personnel throughout the country, one can pick his climate, his season and his city. We know of a young matron who always had a yen to live in the sun. After her children were grown and her husband was free of his business, she invested a few months of her time in a well-known hotel training school and was then in a position to realize her dream. Upon completion of the course, she was able to obtain a position as executive housekeeper in a luxurious Florida hotel. Along with the delightful Florida weather and an adequate salary, she also received a lovely apartment large enough to house herself and her husband plus a nine-weeks' paid vacation. She describes her job as mainly administrative. Her responsibilities consist of coping with knotty personnel problems and maintaining the attractive appearance of the hotel as a home away from home. She hires and fires maids and housemen, trains new personnel for her department, keeps employee records and attends to the purchase of new equipment. Although her course helped her and probably was the reason that she was hired, her experience in running her own home was indispensable.

Another area of the hotel world which is always rewarding is that of hostess or social director. Although the responsibilities differ with hotel or motel, the basic duty of the hostess is to make sure the guests are as comfortable and as happy as possible. It is the "hostess'" job to plan entertainment, advise guests about the activities in the community and serve as a general "new-old" friend. The job can be extremely diversified and stimulating. One woman who had a position as a social director of a Pacific Coast resort hotel told us that her job included introducing congenial guests, helping to prepare special birthday or wedding parties, and arranging entertainment that ran the gamut from cook-outs to goat races.

For the administrative jobs in the field such as personnel director, manager, assistant manager, etc., formal training is required. However, promotion from within is not ruled out, and there are many cases where the assistant housekeeper found herself managing the entire hotel in a short space of years.

More information can be obtained by writing to the American Hotel and Motel Association, 221 W. 57 St., New York, N.Y., 10019 and also the National Executive Housekeepers Association, Inc., Kettering Memorial Hospital, 3535 Southern Blvd., Kettering, Ohio, 45643. For courses in your city, consult your local director of Vocational Education or Superintendent of Schools, or the State Director of Vocational Education, Department of Education in your state capital, and check correspondence courses.

Selling

To market—to market . . . Whether you sell a product, a service or even a home, the same principles apply. Because there are so many areas of selling which are opening up to women, a prospective job seeker should study this huge field closely before making her career choice.

Real Estate

Real estate offers and will continue to offer greater and greater opportunities. As the population booms, the need for suitable shelter will increase. Real estate agents and buyers now realize that a woman showing a house can often be more knowledgeable and per-

DEVELOP A TECHNICAL SKILL

suasive than a man. After all, she does know what a woman wants in a home, and generally what the wife wants turns out to be the most important factor in the purchase. Age is definitely not a detrimental factor in getting into the field. The average age is higher than in most professions. Incomes can be relatively high since there is a five or six percent commission on each piece of property sold by the agent owner, and about half of that if sold by the agent's employees. But don't be too optimistic about immediate high returns; commissions take time to come in. In the beginning it may be necessary for you to carry yourself from six months to a year until you have a backlog of commissions. This can become a severe strain on a meager budget.

Mrs. G. is one case in point. Recently widowed, she cast about for a job in a field that would interest her. She noticed that a good number of new families were constantly moving into her area, and decided that real estate might be a good investment. She armed herself with several courses, took the required license examination and applied for a job with a local broker. Since her commission as the salesperson would be about two and one-half percent, Mrs. G. felt that she could "average out" to at least one thousand dollars a month by making two sales of houses at twenty thousand dollars apiece, per month. Alas, Mrs. G. had not reckoned on the unpredictability of human nature, as well as the fact that people look long and hard before making a decision. She soon realized that novices, even with some training, have a lot to learn in the field.

At the end of six months, Mrs. G. was about ready to toss in the sponge and look for another career. But again, the unpredictable happened, and three "deals" came through. After that, there was a steady sale of homes, and Mrs. G., encouraged by her success, applied for her own broker's license. She is now extremely successful, and has a staff of about six salespeople. In describing the personality traits that make for the most successful real estate salesperson, Mrs. G. looks for maturity, integrity, enthusiasm and an ability to withstand the frustrating complications of a "people" business. One must also be able to act boldly when action is called for, keep a steady nerve in a financial crisis, and have the patience to sweat out long unrewarding periods of "no sale."

Colleges, high schools and vocational schools offer training to the prospective broker and salesperson. Since the field is not yet highly professionalized, it is still possible to get a job with a local real estate broker, who might be willing to "break you in." More information may be obtained from the Real Estate Commission located in your state capital. Most states furnish pamphlets which help to prepare you for the written examination necessary to earn a license. Real estate courses are frequently sponsored by local real estate boards which are members of the National Association of Real Estate Boards. Courses in this subject are also available in private business schools, colleges, universities and correspondence programs. The courses equip the student with the practical know-how of buying and selling real estate, real estate appraisal, law, financing, principles, practices and insurance.

For additional information on opportunities in the field as well as a list of colleges and universities offering real estate courses, write to the Department of Education, National Association of Real Estate Boards, 36

S. Wabash Ave., Chicago, Ill., 60603. Also, correspondence courses are offered in this subject. For more information, write to Robert V. Noble, Head of Correspondence Study, Division of General Education, Florida Institute for Continuing General Studies, SVA, Seagle Bldg., Gainsville, Florida, 32601; Mrs. Larem Coffman, Assistant for Correspondence Study, Room 204, Ad O Bldg., U. of Idaho, SVA, Moscow, Idaho, 83843; Charles W. Hartsell, Director, University Correspondence, The University of Tennessee, QVA, Knoxville, Tenn., 37916.

Insurance

Selling insurance is no longer exclusively a man's job. Unlikely as the idea may seem at first glance, there is sound business sense in woman-to-woman selling. The prospective buyer now feels free to voice her fears about early widowhood, the problems of living alone, etc., to an understanding counterpart. When the woman selling the insurance also demonstrates a complete understanding of the function of insurance, much of the buyer's anxiety about and fear of future planning and working with figures may be dispelled.

A highly successful woman we know entered the insurance field as a result of her husband's death. He had been a successful life insurance agent, and always enjoyed and respected his career. Although she was financially comfortable, she found her days long and dreary. Her only outlet was in answering the phone calls that her husband's old customers and friends made after they ran into snags and wanted some advice about insurance problems. Because she had lived with insurance the better part of her adult life, she found that she could answer any question put to her, and could also advise a young couple about proper insurance purchase. One of her friends called to thank her for the advice she had given to a recently married son and suggested she get a license and go into the business. She was staggered by the idea, but the thought would not leave her. When she investigated, she found that it would indeed be possible. She is now almost equalling her husband's salary and doesn't have a free moment to be depressed or anxious. Needless to say, she is ten years younger in looks and outlook.

It is not difficult to get an insurance license. Some companies require a college degree, while others will consider a high school diploma plus further education at insurance institutes, conferences and seminars. These are generally run by the insurance company itself. The combination of the proper education and experience will qualify you for membership in the American Society of Chartered Life Underwriters. The tests given by the Society apply to knowledge of life insurance, fundamentals of insurance, economics, business law, taxation, trusts and finances.

For the selling of property and casualty insurance, training can be obtained through the Insurance Institute of America, as well as through the American Institute for Property and Liability Underwriters, Inc. A fully qualified person then receives the title, Charter Property Casualty Underwriter.

For more information on both life and casualty insurance selling, write to: Insitute of Life Insurance, 488 Madison Ave., New York, N.Y., 10022; Life Insurance Agency Management Association, 170 Sigourney St., Hartford, Conn., 06105; The National Association of Life Underwriters, 1922 F St., N.W., Washington, D.C.,

20006; Insurance Information Institute, 110 William St., New York, N.Y., 10038; National Association of Insurance Agents, Inc., 96 Fulton St., New York, N.Y., 10038, and the Insurance Institute of America, Inc., 270 Bryn Mawr Ave., Bryn Mawr, Pa., 19010.

General

There is little that is mysterious about the selling job. Most women fall into this role naturally as a result of the many years of coaxing junior to eat spinach, helping Susan to make up her mind about which dress to buy and diplomatically keeping the family peace. If you think back over the years, you will realize you have spent a great deal of time convincing other people to do various things. What you have been doing actually, is practicing a form of selling. Selling is little more than presenting the item, discussing it intelligently, and helping the customer to make up his or her mind whether or not to buy. The days of the hard dynamic "sell," pressuring the mild-mannered customer into panic-buying, have all but vanished. If you are selling a nationally advertised product, much of the initial sales pitch is performed in advance. In selling a ready-to-wear item, you must satisfy the customer or after further consideration she will bring it back the next day. If you are selling in a variety store, your only duty may be to wrap up the items and take the cash. Whatever the selling job, one of its many advantages is that it is one of the few occupations that requires little or no training. It is work that can usually be had on a full-time, part-time or temporary basis. It is also a job in which you will have the opportunity to meet new people daily.

About half the selling jobs in all fields fall into retail

sales. The other areas are broken up into wholesale sales, manufacturers' representatives (sales representatives), insurance, real estate, and other non-classified sales. The field most responsive to women employees is in the retail area. Two out of every five workers in retail sales are women. As long as the economy remains healthy, it is safe to predict that there will be a constant demand for more and more salespeople. With shopping centers sprouting in every suburban community, there is little doubt that a woman who wants a sales position can find one within a few minutes of her door.

Whether the business is a two-man shop or a large department store, the need for a salesperson is always present. Most organizations prefer that their sales help be high school graduates, as well as have articulate and pleasant personalities. Neatness of dress, a friendly manner and an ability to communicate easily are the qualities stressed. Retail selling may require no further knowledge than learning how to write out a sales slip and make change, to the complicated procedure of selling a piano or a home appliance product, where demonstration may be necessary. Often the customer wants to know what materials and product have been used in constructing the item he is interested in purchasing as well as how it works. The qualified salesperson is equipped with this knowledge. The more information the salesperson has about a specific item, the easier it is to make a sale.

It is definitely not true that the behind-the-counter job is a dead end. Many department stores consider selling an excellent training ground for future store executives. Women who have proved proficient at sell-

DEVELOP A TECHNICAL SKILL

ing are often found to be equally successful at buying or administrating. Such job growth is not at all improbable and is in fact highly possible. We visited with Mrs. K., personnel director of a large department store, and as usual were curious as to how she started her career. She told us that she was widowed in her early thirties. She had two pre-teenage children when her husband died. Since she had married directly after graduation from high school, she had absolutely no work or skills background to fall back on. Faced with finding a job that would support herself and her children and still allow her some time with her youngsters, Mrs. K. turned to part-time sales. She did this work for several years until the children were self-sufficient enough to take care of themselves after school. When she suggested to her manager that she would be ready for full-time work, she was immediately promoted to section manager, since her part-time work had been so exceptional. It was soon discovered that she had an unusual knack for training new salespeople, and she was promoted to the job of training new employees. From then on, it was an easy step to personnel and thence to personnel manager. The promotions came along at times when she most needed them, for her promotion to personnel manager coincided with her eldest daughter's acceptance into an out-of-town college. Foresighted action dispersed the agonizing self-pity she felt after her husband died, and helped her to face life bravely in the years that followed.

Although salaries usually start at the minimum wage level in retailing positions, the enterprising person can build up his sales record so that the added commissions will bring his salary up considerably. The average weekly salary is about $75 in large cities—a bit less in smaller communities. A salary as high as $150 a week in certain kinds of sales positions is not unusual. Further information on careers in retailing may be obtained by writing to the Committee on Careers in Retailing, National Retail Merchants Association, 100 West 31 St., New York, N.Y., 10001.

In addition to retail sales, there are also openings for women in the manufacturers' representative area. At present writing, while only ten percent of these manufacturers' "reps" are women, this is not a discouraging figure, for ten percent constitutes about 50,000 workers. Many of the manufacturers in the women's and children's apparel field feel that a woman makes a better representative than a man. A woman knows what a woman likes, and has an instinct for what will be in demand (See Chapter IX for further information).

Another area largely dominated by women reps is food products. Although in some cases a degree as a home economist is required, it is not always essential. If a company can train women to demonstrate and represent its products without too great an expense, the company will more than likely waive the college degree.

Nevertheless, these jobs are more difficult to come by than the ever-present retail job. The best way to gain more information as to the availability of the job is to check with local manufacturers and inquire whether such openings exist. You might write to some of the larger companies that particularly interest you, and suggest that you would like to represent them in your community.

DEVELOP A TECHNICAL SKILL

Cosmetology

Beauty is everyone's business. From the tot whose hair receives special care to the silver-haired great grandmother, the cult of looking one's best is practically a national pastime. The quest for beauty reaches into the animal kingdom as well. Canine parlors in exclusive sections of large cities cater exclusively to the highly endowed poodle—shaving, cutting, clipping and bowing to an inch of a dog's life. Though we do not suggest you become a dog beautician, we do recommend strongly the beauty field as a lucrative, stable career possibility.

With a minimum of specialized education (a high school diploma isn't even necessary), you can learn to be a beauty operator. Every city, town, village and hamlet has its quota of operators. Many enterprising women have used space in their home to set up shop and have become extremely successful. Others, after the required training, have been able to find work in the local beauty salons. Wherever you live, it is likely that once you have developed talent for beautifying the human animal, you will be justly rewarded.

There's not one of us who has not visited a beauty parlor at least once in her life, and marveled at the skilled fingers coaxing the hair into puffs, curls, ringlets, waves or whatever suits the latest fashion. A full-fledged cosmetologist is trained to perform a variety of beauty tasks. She will be expected to give permanent waves and cuts, style, shampoo, straighten, bleach or tint the hair. She will also know how to give manicures; may be trained in scalp and facial treatments.

FROM KITCHEN TO CAREER

She might study the facial contours and skin tones so that she can advise on makeup, and might even become an expert on tinting eyebrows and eyelashes.

Private schools and often a public vocational school are a ready source for beauty culture instruction. Most states require that beauty operators be licensed, and about three-fourths of the states have a reciprocal licensing policy. Depending upon the choice of school, the course may last from nine months to three years. Obviously, the longer and more intensive the study, the greater will be your skill and knowledge, and ultimately your earning power. Both the public and private school training includes classroom study, demonstrations and practical application. In the beginning, students practice on each other. After some skill is attained, they are transferred into beauty clinics and gain experience on actual customers who pay only a modest sum for their beauty treatment.

It is difficult to estimate the number of jobs for beauty operators which open each year, but it is known that there are literally thousands of vacancies. Most operators work either for themselves or for small beauty salons. It is equally difficult to estimate the earnings of the beauty operators. A common starting salary is about $55 a week, but if one includes the tips, the salary would be closer to $100 a week. Some beauticians specializing in extremely creative work have been known to earn as much as $300 a week. Another customary arrangement may be to receive a small basic salary plus a commission ranging from forty to fifty percent.

More information on careers will be sent by the National Hairdressers and Cosmetologists Association,

DEVELOP A TECHNICAL SKILL

175 Fifth Ave., New York, N.Y., 10010. A list of approved schools may be had by writing to the National Association of Cosmetology Schools, Inc., 3839 White Plains Road, New York, N.Y., 10067.

Fashion

Affectionately called the "rag trade" by its more intimate members, the field of fashion is limitless. It is a field where the novice can become a world celebrity overnight by presenting a startling new style which catches on. It is a field in which the untrained as well as the fully experienced can, and often do, make fabulous fortunes. It is a field that glitters, glows and will use every ounce of imagination that a person can muster. It is an old field, dating probably from the donning of woman's first dress. Plautus, when he described his Roman women in antiquity had them fretting about the lack of something suitable to wear. The trait seems to be as old as it is human.

Design Your Way to Fame

That something-suitable-to-wear has launched many a woman on a fashion designing career. We heard of a couple of young matrons who could not find a tennis dress to their liking. Although they lived in a large metropolis, the tennis dresses they were shown were either too expensive or terribly unflattering—so they designed their own. The result was so electrifying that all of their friends pleaded with them for outfits equally as flattering. These two young matrons, who incidentally have three and four children each, not only fulfilled the needs of the neighborhood, but kept expanding and succeeding. They worked up a series of sample dresses and presented them to the merchandising manager of a large New York department store. They landed the order, although at the time of presentation, they were so nervous they almost did not keep the appointment. Not too long ago, our enterprising matrons proudly announced that their tennis dresses were being promoted and sold in fifty better shops throughout the country.

Generally, the housewife who launches into a fashion career does so by accident rather than by direction. It is not likely that she will sit down and design an item that will have large market value, and will also be inexpensive enough to manufacture in order to compete with the products already on the market. But when a woman can sew, she is generally making things for herself that suit her particular taste and need. One young woman was launched on her career solely because she found it exceedingly difficult to find well-styled clothes in her tiny size. Another woman designed easy-to-wear dresses while helping out in her husband's business. Everybody wanted to buy the dress, rather than the product her husband was selling. Some women have found that in sewing for their children they were able to design and sell girls' dresses for which there is a decided fashion market. The motto of the designing end of fashion seems to be, if you do not find what you want, design it! If people try to tear the clothes you made off your back, you have an item that will go!

If you plan to start making an item of clothing, begin on a small scale! Investment in machinery and materials can be very costly. Most of the women we described began in their basements or spare rooms, and as the business grew, they expanded. Remember that the average housewife does not have the money to spend on promotion and advertising. Therefore, your item will have to grow through word of mouth and general store promotion. However, do not be discouraged! New and better mousetraps are always in demand. And if you happen to be one of those people whose creativity and imagination are unlimited, keep sewing and you cannot fail.

Buying and Selling

Suppose you are the kind of shopper who can read trends and can choose a garment that looks like a million but costs very little—then you might best be suited for the fashion shop. Many women, confused by the large department store where racks and racks of the same type of dresses hang on display, seek out the small specialty shop. The impersonality of the store and its salespeople tends to frighten away a large part of the market. A small shop where the garments are carefully selected can prove a boon to the intrepid but weary shopper. We know of one young widow in her late thirties who was shopping for a wedding dress for her second marriage. She haunted the large department stores, looking desperately for the right kind of dress. Exhausted after several weeks of fruitless searching, she passed a neighborhood shop and saw just the dress casually displayed in the window. The price was even lower than for some of the so-called "better-store" dresses, and the shop fitted the dress perfectly at no extra charge. The time and energy saved plus the excellent selection of clothes offered made a confirmed customer out of this woman. An interest in fashion, a small amount of capital, and you too can set up shop in your neighborhood. Customers will come if your prices are geared to neighborhood demand, and your styles are geared to the tastes in your community.

Often, zoning and apartment laws allow the owner or renter to conduct business at home. If you wish to start your own dress or sportswear business, it is usually wiser to begin small. Dipping your toes in, then fully immersing yourself may reveal many of the facts of the business world to you, without your having to undergo a total commitment of capital and time. For example, you may find that you do not like to play the role of saleswoman, but do enjoy the buying—or vice-versa. You may be the kind of person who likes to be busy all the time, and many little shops have lean periods during the day as well as during the season. Test it out first before taking the plunge. An excellent way to find out is to work for a small shop owner and try to learn store operation.

Modeling

This is another fashion outlet that the more mature woman can try. Of course, the field is limited; but even for the twenty-year-old the field is limited. The same rules hold for the mature model as for the youngster. Good looks, trim figure, winning and photogenic personality. Advertisers have found that it is refreshing to use a mature model in roles where a mature person is traditional.

Fashion Coordinators

These are people who usually stage fashion shows. They do exactly what their title implies. They put together an outfit from shoes to hat. They sometimes design the backdrop of a fashion stage and even develop the full pageant. It is somewhat difficult to crash the big city fashion coordinating market, but many women have been exceedingly successful in small towns. Since fashion is such a large encompassing field, there is no direct source where you get additional information. The Fashion Institute of Technology, 227 W. 27 St., New York, N.Y. does, however, have pamphlets available on apparel and design, textile design, fashion illustration, advertising and interior design. We also suggest that you check your local library since a great many books have been written on the field of fashion.

Interior Decorating

This field can be extraordinarily exciting for the imaginative woman who is intensely interested in home furnishings. If you are the kind of person who enjoys meeting many people, solving problems, never having a minute to yourself, and using every ounce of your creative imagination, the field of interior decoration may be for you.

It is still possible to enter this field without a college degree. The number of jobs is limited, but it is to the credit of the highly imaginative women who really enjoy the field that so many of them nowadays are able to own part-time interior decorating businesses. We know of two young matrons in the metropolitan area who developed a fine following while raising their respective children. They met while taking a course at one of the design schools. They pooled their resources and their clients—both rather minimal—and set to work to prove that they could operate an *haute decor* business on a low-cost furnishing budget. When they first began their unusual partnership, they inveigled their friends to give them free access to recently acquired living quarters. The young contemporaries of our neophyte designers were in the midst of marrying or moving out to the suburbs. Experience rather than money was what these two women wanted. Their friends found the attraction of buying wholesale, plus having free consultation on home furnishings irresistible. They gave *carte blanche*, and our two decorators went to work. The results were so eye-catching and the cost of the furnishings was so moderate, that success was almost immediate.

Decorating from the home living room tends to be a business that is largely developed through word-of-mouth advertising. The satisfied customer tells another person, and soon the decorator has a host of clients in need of her services. To be a good decorator, it is important to have an excellent knowledge of every area of home furnishings, together with a superb sense of color. Obviously, you must be able to recognize at a glance the difference between Italian and French Provincial; styles of furniture dating back to the twelfth century; architectural developments, etc. However, even as you dip into antiquity, one part of your mind must be searching for the newest design trends. Selection of fabrics and rugs calls for the same wide knowledge. An eye for line, color and detail is perhaps the most essential asset. A knowledge of where to buy and where the price is lowest is also important. A good decorator must be able to evaluate the construction of a piece of furniture, and to sublimate her own tastes to fully empathize with the tastes of her client. If a decorator prefers modern, and her client prefers traditional, then traditional the furnishings will be.

DEVELOP A TECHNICAL SKILL

Often decorating is a balancing act involving decorator versus wife, and husband versus wife. The decorator convinces the wife of the soundness of purchasing certain items; the wife in turn convinces the husband; then the purchase is made. Although there are many men in the interior design field, decorating and choosing furniture still seem to fall into the female domain. One reason there are so many women in the field may be that a woman can serve two or three clients, and handle the work on a part-time basis. What she earns is considered supplemental to the family income. When a man enters the field, he usually does it as an interior designer, combining decorating and the actual design of furniture and fixtures. In order to be financially successful and gain a large following of clients, he usually finds that he must put in a number of years of extensive training. Expensive college training, as we know, very often limits the number of professionals in a field.

Earnings in the field vary considerably according to location and amount of time spent on the job. Most qualified and reputable decorators get a consulting fee, plus a small commission on the furniture purchased. Since the furniture is bought at wholesale prices, the client still receives better quality for the amount of money paid.

Training can vary from one or two courses in interior decorating to a fully accredited four-year course with any of the design schools, colleges or correspondence programs. For those women who want to make decorating a truly professional career, the zenith is membership in either the American Institute of Interior Design or the National Society of Interior Designers. Requirements for membership are four years of education beyond high school with major emphasis on design, plus several years of experience. More information can be obtained by writing to the American Institute of Interior Designers, 673 Fifth Ave., New York 10022, and the National Society of Interior Designers, Inc., Suite 700, 157 W. 57 St., New York, N.Y. 10019.

Another area where a decorating instinct can be made to pay off is in designing an item and selling either the finished piece or the idea to manufacturers or retail stores. A young Brazilian woman who was on the verge of a divorce found herself doodling away at furniture design to keep her mind off her immediate problems. She had studied art at college some ten years ago and thus knew the fundamentals of design and drafting. As she played around with shapes, she discovered that she was coming up with furniture ideas. She showed her drawings to a few architects who had also been dabbling in design ideas. Together they pooled their concepts and money to develop a furniture trend that was to revolutionize the middle-income market in Brazil. The furniture was modern, reasonably priced and completely coordinated. It was possible to furnish an entire house with units that integrated with each other. At that time in Brazil, the only furniture equaling these designs in taste and quality was scandalously expensive imports from the Scandinavian countries. So convinced were the designers that they had something worthwhile, that despite the fact that they had a bank account of approximately one dollar when they opened shop, they were not panicked. The ideas were so good that the business is now a smashing success.

A decorating talent or flair may be put to useful purpose in designing lamps and lampshades. Also, some women find that they are adept at making slipcovers and draperies for which neighbors are willing to pay. Other women may find that they are able to produce interesting ceramic pieces. Any item that will add beauty to homemaking will find its way into the decorator's repertoire. If you are artistic, why not try to create some useful and practical objects? Even making designer pillows can be an excellent way to bring extra cash into the house, without heavy expenditure in time and money.

Don't be afraid to explore your ideas. And do not let friends discourage you. Many of today's most successful products were first regarded as sure failures. Even the now successful *New Yorker* magazine when first launched was labeled by experts as doomed to fail. There is no accounting for taste. And if you think you have something that is right and useful, go ahead and make or design it. You will never succeed if you don't try—so let the public be your judge.

Drive Your Own Cab

And make money doing it! If you are the kind of woman who is complimented on her ability to drive like a man, you might want to investigate the possibility of driving a cab. We note that more and more women are invading this traditionally male occupation. If you are a skilled driver you have practically all the requirements. In addition to your driver's license, you need a chauffeur's license—which involves a somewhat stiffer driving test—and you also need a special taxicab operator's license, which is issued by the local police, safety department, or Public Utilities Commission.

You can either drive your own cab, or work for an organization.

We were curious to know why some women preferred driving cabs to the more feminine forms of work. After interviewing several of the metropolitan female cabbies, we found that usually a woman was drawn to this kind of work because she could not bear to be enclosed in an office or store. Generally, she had little income to spend on further training. Selling or clerical work seemed too confining. She generally admitted that she was happiest when she was out and driving. We asked these women if they ever had difficulty with male passengers. None of them reported excessive problems. Some said they would not take a fare to a deserted area of town. Others recounted how they invented tales and gimmicks that would dampen growing ardor. One woman said: "I always tell them that my kid is sick in the hospital and I've got loads of bills to pay. This always gets them, and they leave a bigger tip." From what we can gather, cabbing seems to be for the free-spirited, intrepid woman who has a lot of energy and little fear of operating on her own. Salaries including tips run from about $75 to $100 a week, depending upon the number of hours worked.

Placement Manager

Most good-sized cities and towns have at least several private employment agencies. The qualifications for a placement manager can range from an untrained but sympathetic individual to a highly trained psychologist. These positions are unique in that the more mature person very often makes the best placement manager, that skills other than warmth, perseverance

DEVELOP A TECHNICAL SKILL

and a high frustration tolerance are not necessary, and that successful managers can earn an exceedingly high income.

To be a good placement manager, you must be able to determine a person's goals and to direct these goals into marketability. You also must have the perseverance to explore the market continually for job opportunities, initiate special promotional campaigns and be quick-thinking.

A good placement manager is not born—she is made through long hours and hard work. But the gratification is there. Whether you place the young or old, the professional or the trainee, the thrill of fitting somebody in that perfect niche is tremendously fulfilling. Be prepared, however, to work on either a low salary or a commission basis. High earnings can be had, but the income depends entirely upon your own efforts.

CHAPTER IX | *A Business Of Your Own*

Ingenuity, elbow grease and some capital—put them all together, and you may be making the Great American dream come true. Not only is starting your own business very possible, it can also be very profitable. No one need be frightened by the giant corporations swallowing up business after business; American ingenuity is apparently always busy creating new markets faster than the corporation monster can digest the old. Automation notwithstanding, the need for personalized services in many households continues to create new demands and new machines run by individuals to take care of these demands. With all the mass-produced products on the market, the made-at-home item can still be a best seller and a money maker.

The old stand-bys of small business operation from home such as making jellies, dressmaking, various forms of sewing and mending are always a possibility. It is always true—a job well done can often create from a dull idea a startling new concept. For example, we know of one not-young-at-all lady (when we met her, she must have been eighty) who opened up a tiny shop to vend her jams and jellies. Her pride in her product was immense, similar to the pride that a vintner takes in his wines. She would discuss the quality of the Damson plums, the raspberries and strawberries that year and indicate which harvest had been exceptional. Her jams and jellies were a delight, so good that her identification scratchings on the bottle tops added to the aura of quaintness, gentility and quality.

Another lady we knew whose husband was a struggling playwright decided to earn extra money from sewing. She merely put a sign in her window announcing her existence and within a few weeks, people began to give her projects. With the huge ready-to-wear market, it was quite amazing how many people were eager to use her services. Many women buy material with the intention of making up a very special dress. More often than not, the time never comes for that special project, nor does the woman really have the skill to tackle a fine garment. If a little dressmaker around the corner is able to create her design at a moderate price, our lady is delighted; she tells her friends and comes back for more.

But skills need not be the only means of making money at home. We recently read in the *New York Times* that a woman was developing a profitable business by renting homes in Europe to Americans who preferred to stay in one spot rather than travel around. The business grew from her own inability to find an organization set up to rent her a home in Europe. From her own investigations, she was able to find several homes where owners were pleased to "rent out." She now has a partner in Europe who investigates each house before it is added to her list of over one hundred.

The rents range from about $450 to $5000 for three months. For this service, she receives a fee, adequate to meet her expenses and bring her a sound profit.

The profitable things a woman can do in her own backyard are almost too numerous to mention. Almost any skill, any idea, any ability can be turned to advantage. Many women have made jewelry, leather bags and belts and ceramic pieces in their home. A young woman who made some earrings out of mink on a dare found herself deluged with orders. Often, your own skill or ability is the key to the kind of business that would be both stimulating and profitable to you. However, if you are stymied, if all ideas seem worthless, then it might be well to look into other sources for help and guidance.

A government organization called the Small Business Administration is set up specifically for you, the projected business owner. It will answer your questions, advise you on business problems and help you to determine whether or not you belong in business. For example, it would certainly be wise before making a large business investment to question yourself closely. Some of the questions the Small Business Administration asks are:

Are you the type?

> Rate your personal traits such as leadership, organizing ability, perseverance, and physical energy.
>
> Now have your friends rate them.

Chances for success

> Any business experience?
>
> Have you analyzed the need in your neighborhood?

A BUSINESS OF YOUR OWN

Have you determined the size business you want to establish?

Do you have an idea of the capital to be invested?

Do you know the break-even point?

How much capital will you need?

Can you afford an uneven income for several months or years?

Do you have assets that you can borrow on?

Will the income you make be less than, comparable to or greater than working for somebody else?

Have you discussed the financial details with a banker, a lawyer and your husband?

Do you have reserve should you need to invest more capital?

Should you go into partnership?

Would a friend with skills you do not have add to the growth of the business?

Do you need financial assistance that a partner could bring?

Location

Have you checked into all the suitable locations?

How much space will you need?

Can the business be started from your home—your basement, your back-yard?

Have you checked the U. S. Census Bureau population figures?

Selling methods

What selling methods will you use?

Do you have a sales policy?

Would outside selling trouble you?

Would you have the capital to advertise in the newspapers?

Would you consider door-to-door selling if necessary?

Would you be able to do direct mail advertising?

Would you use local radio and television stations for advertising?

Price of product or services

Have you determined what prices you will have to charge to cover your costs and obtain profits?

Will the price you have fixed compare favorably with your competitors?

How will you manage personnel?

Will you be able to find skilled help in your vicinity should you need to expand?

Have you checked the prevailing wage scale?

Do you feel you will be able to train a new employee?

Record keeping

Will you be able to keep the books, or will you have to hire a bookkeeper to assist you?

Have you planned a merchandise control system?

Have you a system to use in keeping a check on costs?

Will you need any special forms?

Are you familiar with the records necessary for local, state or federal government regulations?

What laws will affect you?

Have you investigated whether you will need a license to run your proposed business. If you do need a license, do you have the qualifications for obtaining said license?

Have you checked health regulations?

Are your operations subject to interstate commerce regulations?

Have you checked with your lawyer?

Miscellaneous problems that may arise

Have you worked out a system for handling your tax requirements?

Do you have adequate insurance coverage?

Is your family behind you?

Do you have enough capital to carry your accounts receivable?

Will you sell for credit?

Have you worked out a definite returned goods policy?

Have you set up a work plan?

Have you made a plan for keeping up with new developments in your line of business?

Can you turn to anybody in the business for advice?

If the above questions do not terrify you, then you might begin thinking about opening up your own business. The Small Business Administration (consult page 151 for office nearest you) has produced a booklet that will give you the answers to these and any other questions you may have. These booklets provide valuable information on all phases of business operation. Some of them are free of charge; others may be purchased at minimal expense. You probably will need capital if you plan to start a small business. The Small Business Administration, your local bank and loan organizations can assist you in obtaining capital. The Social Security Administration offers a special booklet on information for self-employed people. It is wise to send for this before you open your doors.

The Small Business Administration also runs a one-day workshop for prospective business owners. Here you can talk to experts about the problems that face you as an individual. People with backgrounds in accounting, mechanics, sales, engineering, as well as housewives and students have attended this workshop successfully. The workshops are designed to give some basic idea of what it means to run a business. There are sessions on financial requirements, the selection of a location, the organization of your business, taxes and business regulations, the buying of an existing business, the management requirements of your business, the ingredients of a good owner-manager, where to go for advice and assistance. More information can be obtained by writing to your nearest Small Business Administration office.

Investment—Warily ... Wisely ... Watchfully

No doubt a great deal of money can be made by investing in a business. We all know the old adage that money begets money. If you have several thousand dollars, and you prefer to invest it in some business, proceed cautiously. Too many people have found a company to be a hoax only after their hard-earned dollars are lost forever. There are many organizations which are interested in setting up franchises all over the country. When you choose a franchise, be sure to investigate the company thoroughly. It is wiser to spend a few hundred dollars initially than to lose a few thousand after some painful months of disillusionment.

Franchises that could be handled by women may be roughly divided into three categories: food, home care and cleaning, and entertainment. The food franchise

A BUSINESS OF YOUR OWN

SMALL BUSINESS ADMINISTRATION LISTING OF FIELD OFFICE ADDRESSES

* BOSTON, MASSACHUSETTS 02210
- Sheraton Building
  470 Atlantic Avenue
- Augusta, Maine 04330
  114 Western Ave.
- Concord, New Hampshire 03301
  DuBois Building
  72 North Main Street
- Montpelier, Vermont 05601
  79 Main North Street
- Providence, Rhode Island 02903
  611 Smith Building
  57 Eddy Street

* NEW YORK, NEW YORK 10004
  42 Broadway
- ▲ Buffalo, New York 14203
  448 Ellicott Sq. Bldg.
  295 Main St.
- Hartford, Connecticut 06103
  Federal Office Bldg.
  450 Main St.
- Santurce, Puerto Rico 00908
  San Alberto Condominio Bldg.
  1200 Ponce de Leon Avenue
- Syracuse, New York 13202
  Chimes Building
  500 So. Salina Street
- ▲ St. Thomas, U. S. Virgin Islands 00802
  P. O. Box 806

* PHILADELPHIA, PENNSYLVANIA 19107
  Jefferson Building
  1015 Chestnut Street
- Pittsburgh, Pennsylvania 15222
  Fulton Building
  107 6th Street

* RICHMOND, VIRGINIA 23226
- P. O. Box 8565
  1904 Byrd Ave.
- Baltimore, Maryland 21202
  521 Calvert Building
  Fayette & St. Paul Streets
- Charleston, West Virginia 25301
  3000 U. S. Court House & Fed. Bldg.
  500 Quarrier Street
- Charlotte, North Carolina 28202
  Cutter Building
  201 S. Tryon Street
- Clarksburg, West Virginia 26301
  Old Post Office Building
  227 West Pike Street
- Columbia, South Carolina 29201
  1801 Assembly Street
- Washington, D. C. 20416
  726 Jackson Place, N. W.

* ATLANTA, GEORGIA 30303
  90 Fairlie St., N. W.

FROM KITCHEN TO CAREER

- Birmingham, Alabama 35203
 New 1st Fed. Savings & Loan Bldg.
 2030 1st Avenue North
- Jackson, Mississippi 39201
 322 U. S. Post Office & Courthouse Bldg.
 Capital & West Sts.
- Jacksonville, Florida 32202
 47 West Forsyth
- Knoxville, Tennessee 37902
 233 West Cumberland Bldg.
 301 West Cumberland Ave.
- Miami, Florida 33131
 301 Huntington Building
 168 Southeast First Street
- Nashville, Tennessee 37219
 Security Federal Savings & Loan Bldg.
 500 Union Street

* CLEVELAND, OHIO 44113
 Standard Building
 1370 Ontario Street
- Colmbus, Ohio 43215
 Beacon Building
 50 West Gay Street
- Louisville, Kentucky 40202
 1900 Commonwealth Building
 Fourth and Broadway

* CHICAGO, ILLINOIS 60603
 430 Bankers Building
 105 West Adams Street
- Des Moines, Iowa 50309
 850 Insurance Exchange Bldg.
 Fifth and Grand Avenue
- Indianapolis, Indiana 46204
 721 Farm Bureau Insurance Building
 130 East Washington Street

- Madison, Wisconsin 53703
 Commercial State Bank Building
 114 North Carroll Street

* MINNEAPOLIS, MINNESOTA 55402
- Lewis Building
 603 Second Ave. South
- Fargo, North Dakota 58102
 300 American Life Bldg.
 207 North Fifth Street
- Sioux Falls, South Dakota 57102
 Leaders Building
 109½ North Main Avenue

* KANSAS CITY, MISSOURI 64106
 911 Walnut Street
- Omaha, Nebraska 68102
 7425 Federal Building
 215 North 17th Street
- St. Louis, Missouri 63103
 2469 Federal Building
 1520 Market Street
- Wichita, Kansas 67202
 215 Board of Trade Building
 120 South Market Street

* DALLAS, TEXAS 75202
- United Fidelity Life Bldg.
 1025 Elm Street
- Houston, Texas 77002
 802 Federal Office Bldg.
 201 Fannin St.
- Little Rock, Arkansas 72201
 377 Post Office and Courthouse Bldg.
 600 W. Capital Avenue
- Lubbock, Texas 79401
 204 Federal Office Building
 1616 19th Street

152

A BUSINESS OF YOUR OWN

- Marshall, Texas 75670
  Marshall National Bank
  101 East Austin Street
- New Orleans,
  Louisiana 70130
  303 Federal Office
  Bldg. (South)
  610 South Street
- Oklahoma City,
  Oklahoma 73102
  807 U. S. Post Office Bldg.,
  3rd and Robinson
- San Antonio, Texas 78204
  412 Kallison Building
  434 So. Main Avenue

* DENVER,
  COLORADO 80202
  Railway Exchange Building
  909 17th Street
- Albuquerque,
  New Mexico 87101
  102 U. S. Courthouse
  Fifth and Gold Streets,
  S. W.
▲ Casper, Wyoming
  P. O. Box 862
- Salt Lake City, Utah 84101
  520 Kearns Building
  136 South Main Street

* SAN FRANCISCO,
  CALIFORNIA 94105
  525 Market Street
▲ Agana, Guam 96910
  P. O. Box 927
- Honolulu, Hawaii 96813
  Finance Factors Building
  195 South King Street

* SEATTLE,
  WASHINGTON 98104
- 1206 Smith Tower
  506 Second Avenue
- Anchorage, Alaska 99501
  5th & D Streets
  P. O. Box 999
- Boise, Idaho 83702
  P. O. Box 933
  214 Sonna Building
  910 Main Street
- Helena, Montana 59601
  P. O. Box 1690
  205 Power Block
  Corner Main & 6th Avenue
- Portland, Oregon 97205
  330 Pittock Block
  921 S. W. Washington St.
- Spokane, Washington 99201
  Post Office and Courthouse
  West 904 Riverside Ave.

* LOS ANGELES,
  CALIFORNIA 90013
  312 W. 5th Street
- Phoenix, Arizona 85004
  Central Towers Building
  2727 No. Central Avenue
▲ San Diego, California 92104
  3969 Ohio St.

* DETROIT,
  MICHIGAN 48226
  232 West Grand
  River Avenue
▲ Marquette, Michigan 49855
  Northern Michigan College
  P. O. Box 912
  Public Service Center Bldg.

* Regional Offices
• Branch Offices
▲ Post of Duty Stations

153

people usually have a brand name and specially designed unit. For your investment, you receive consultation services on the location, cooperative advertising, equipment, signs, etc. You still have to provide the real estate and the building from which you will operate. The company is so organized that you will receive maximum service and maximum information. However, the investment is high, the hours are usually long, and you must have a good notion of how to run a business.

Home care and cleaning offer another form of franchise. Several companies are developing special units to clean rugs, furniture and walls. While the cleaning itself is usually a man's job, the operation of the business could easily be handled by a woman. One company sells the units individually, so the growth of the business and the initial cash outlay can be correlated. In a business such as this, cash to start might not be more than five hundred dollars. A cleaning business, on the other hand, would require a large investment of capital—fifteen to twenty-five thousand dollars. It would be necessary to rent a store, either buy or rent the cleaning equipment, finance the advertising and promotion. Also, when you open a business that employs people other than yourself, it is important to realize that you will need operating capital to cover salaries, taxes and everyday expenses.

The entertainment business is expanding. As people have more and more leisure time, they begin to seek more pastimes to fill these hours. Some companies offer many forms of miniature golf, from putting ranges to electronic golf courses that score whether you hooked, sliced, or "split the fairway." A control panel simulates the actual "fairway" conditions (fast, average or

A BUSINESS OF YOUR OWN

heavy). Other companies concentrate on archery, with life-like targets for real range practice; or billiards where you can establish your own up-to-date billiard parlor. None of these franchises is cheap, for each requires that you purchase a reasonable amount of equipment and have a piece of property where the equipment can be located. But the owners of these organizations will help you to set up and promote your business.

For more information about franchising from the people who are in the business and from the people who have franchised business, you might subscribe to "Modern Franchising," 549 W. Washington St., Chicago 6, Illinois.

A completely unique form of franchising for the person who likes to advise others is Simplified Business Services, Incorporated, which for the past thirty-two years has made a business of keeping small enterprises afloat. This organization not only helps the small businessman to iron out the kinks in his business but also offers a franchise to any qualified person who wants to open shop. Its advice is widespread, ranging from sales tips to a man who tended to oversell, to revamping the approach of a restaurateur who wanted greater efficiency. The organization counseled a fruit store in the Bronx on how to conduct a grand opening, and informed a nursing home on the procedures of holding open house. What the firm really offers is a packaged management consultant service to small business. More information can be gathered from the organization itself: Simplified Business Services, Incorporated, 140 Varick Street, New York, N.Y.

CHAPTER X | *Spare Time Dollars*

Most women have more spare time during the day and evening than they realize. Even with a large family and full household responsibilities, a woman who can organize her day will find the time available to pursue some money-making activity. Most housewives when pressed will admit that dawdling is a household disease. However, a large proportion of the housewives are now beginning to turn their dawdles into dollars.

Home Selling

Home selling is one of the easiest ways to use extra time fruitfully. Here you can choose your own hours. No need to schedule the household chores around the new project; the new project can be scheduled around the housework. It is wise, however, in choosing a product, that you select one that is nationally advertised. Certainly, you do not want to be selling an inferior product to your friends and neighbors. Thoroughly investigate the item before you undertake to be its local representative. Once you have chosen the product that is most interesting to you, get in touch with the company that might be able to employ you. If you can spare four to five hours a day, a company representative will come to train you, equip you with a demonstration portfolio and assign a territory to you. After that although you are on your own, the company always stands behind you.

One of the best items you can sell from your home is cosmetics. One large name brand, Avon, has a literal army of women selling its products. Experienced women can earn well into the five-figure bracket if they are able to put enough time on the job. Or, if you prefer, you can buy cosmetics from a manufacturing concern, which will package the products under your own brand name. If you have visions of becoming another Helena Rubinstein, this might be the way to get a good start. When packaging your own cosmetics, be sure you find a reputable manufacturer. Good quality means return customers.

Companies manufacturing slenderizers, massagers, recliners, and portable steam baths are all seeking representatives. You might even start your own gym in the spare room while you demonstrate to friends and neighbors the satisfaction of owning this type of equipment. Most of these products are definitely designed for home use. They are light, practical and moderately priced. A responsible company will stand behind any product you sell, and in many cases will offer a reasonable warranty.

Other areas of home selling may be in the clothing line. Some women have been known to make sizeable incomes by selling ladies' lingerie from their homes. Other women have set up small dress shops in their apartments or homes. By making careful selection of the merchandise, it is possible to bring a good line of apparel into your living room. We know of one mature lady who turned her living room into a dress shop and has been quite successful in supplying the neighborhood women with beautiful clothes. Because she had no other overhead, she could afford to sell for considerably less money the same dress seen at the major department stores. And further, she offered free alterations. Other sources of income may be gained from selling uniforms, stockings, robes, men's clothing, etc. Almost any item you can name will be marketable, once you have developed a modus operandi.

If your tastes run to the intellectual, it is possible to sell encyclopedias, teaching machines and Great Books. If you are looking for an unusual item, how about a five-year light bulb, carpet squares or a telephone minder? If a Small Business Show comes your way, step in and take a look at the items and franchises offered. Watch the direct mail ads in newspapers and magazines. And always bear in mind—your ingenuity is one of your greatest assets.

Direct Mail/Mail Order

Speaking of assets, we heard of one young woman who began to supplement her husband's income by making rubber stamps. She clipped out an advertisement from the paper telling how a rubber stamp business could pay beginners up to ten dollars an hour. She wrote away for the starter's kit, and within a short time began to make professional rubber stamps. Neighbors, companies and organizations soon heard about her stamps and were especially impressed by the low price she was able to charge. Orders increased. Her husband, who had scoffed at the venture, helped her to fix up a studio in the basement. This young woman was finally able to get that freezer and carpeting that had not seemed possible even after twelve years of marriage.

If you live in an area where there is heavy traffic, you might invest in an ice vending machine. Or you might prefer a milk machine, a cigarette vending machine, cold or hot drinks, newspapers—more are being manufactured every day to take care of the consumer's immediate needs. Your only responsibility is to keep the machine supplied—it does the rest.

Hostess

Other non-selling work that can be done from the home might be as a hostess with a firm such as Welcome Wagon. The hostess welcomes the newcomer to the community by showering her with gifts from local firms. She also tells the newcomer about the shopping centers, schools, hospitals, churches and other community facilities that exist in the area. Sponsoring local firms pay the hostess a fee for this service, and the visits prove to be both profitable and enjoyable for both parties.

A restaurant hostess combines grace, charm and dignity. She reflects the attitude of the restaurant. She guides the diner to his table and makes him feel at home. She helps the waitresses in taking orders and moving the flow of customers from table to table. She is a decided asset to a fine restaurant, for she is the one who helps to set the tone.

The job of hostess is one that naturally falls into the orbit of the more mature woman. It is a job that often requires nothing more than that a person be presentable and have an appealing personality. It need not even call for a high school education, so long as the individual is well-spoken and articulate. Jobs for hostesses are available in most good-sized quality restaurants. In smaller communities, the number of jobs is limited, since there may be only two or three restaurants needing the service of a hostess. The larger the city, the larger the number of hostesses in demand. But do not set your heart on the job of hostess unless you are attractive, have a trim figure and live in a bustling metropolis.

Starting salaries range from about $75 to $100 a week in cities, slightly lower in towns and in the southern part of the United States. Follow up your interest by visiting restaurants in your vicinity, or by watching the newspaper advertisements.

Research Interviewing

This is a stimulating, provocative part-time job that will net a fair-sized salary. Because market research firms take sample interviews from every part of the country, it is possible to become a field interviewer no matter where you live. In essence, the field interviewer is the person who is given a group of questionnaires, and is required to find the suitable respondents for completion of these questionnaires. Top caliber interviewing requires a high level of verbal skill. It is essential that a person be articulate, have a warm outgoing personality, be patient and persistent, but not overbearing. The better the interviewer, the more valid is the information received.

Field interviewing is used to gather information on how the country thinks. Whether the information is about the brand of cigarettes smoked, television ratings, or who will be elected president, the methods of eliciting this information are somewhat similar. Usually, an interviewer is equipped with a questionnaire plus instructions on how the questionnaire should be completed and the manner in which respondents should be selected. If the interview is to determine actual product testing, then the interviewer must also have samples of the products to demonstrate.

When an interviewer is hired, she is usually trained by the field supervisor. The latter is a man or woman who covers a territory. It is his or her job to see that the interviewers are trained, and that each section of the territory is covered.

One young matron told us why she had chosen field interviewing as a part-time occupation when she found it was necessary for her to bring extra money into the home. She wanted a job that would not be on a nine-to-five basis, since her children were still too young to be left alone. She was interested in sculpturing and knew that if she gave up the spare time needed for her avocation she would be miserable. After examining the market, she decided that the job that would give her the most freedom and allow her the maximum time for her family and herself would be interviewing. She began her campaign to get work by writing to the research departments of various universities in her city. She also visited the research departments of advertising agencies and market research companies. She was pleased to find that many of these organizations were interested in the amount of leadership she had displayed on a volunteer basis. Her activities in civic organizations and the PTA paid off. She was given several small jobs, and her performance was so good that she was made a permanent member of the part-time field staff of several research organizations. On a part-time basis she found it possible to earn from $75 to $90 a week.

There is no direct source from which to obtain more information on field interviewing. But since every market research firm and every research department of advertising agencies must cover the country nationally in any survey it runs, you should not find it too difficult to establish contacts by writing directly to several companies. Bear in mind also that most universities run comprehensive studies that spread-eagle the country. The University of Chicago is well known for this type of research. Also watch your local papers. Companies will often advertise directly to recruit a staff necessary for conducting a survey. Finding the interviewing job might take a little ingenuity and spadework on your part, but the results will be well worth it.

CHAPTER XI | *Careers With The Government*

On October 18, 1963, Esther Peterson, Assistant Secretary of Labor, and John W. Macy, Jr., Chairman of the Civil Service Commission, reported on the findings of the President's Commission on the status of women. They reported, for the official record, what we already know—that the American woman is now a woman of two careers. She expects to manage her home as have her mother and her grandmother before her, but she also expects to be allowed to spiral off into a life career of her own. Herself a woman in her mid-thirties, with half her life ahead of her and with the time, talent and the motivation to be productive in the emerging new world of the 1960's, Miss Peterson in her report stressed that the acceptance of the American woman as an individual has increased markedly. Here are some of the significant statistics:

> Increased life expectancy and earlier marriage and child-bearing give the average American woman 30 years after her child care responsibilities are largely completed.
>
> The percentage of women workers of 45 years of age is increasing (normally a woman employed is in her 40's after her

FROM KITCHEN TO CAREER

children have entered school); the average age of employed women is now 41 compared with 26 in 1900.

One worker in three is a woman (presently approximately 24 million women are employed with approximately 30 million forecast for 1970).

Approximately three out of five women workers are married; among married women, one in three is working; among nonwhite women, almost one in two is working.

One out of three non-white mothers with children under the age of six was in the labor force in 1960; one out of five white mothers.

With our government so vitally interested in the progress of the older woman, we should certainly not fail to examine the opportunities available for federal careers. The important consideration to bear constantly in mind is that although many of these careers call for college graduates, it *is* possible to complete your degree while taking care of your home responsibilities (see Chapter V). Although the majority of positions are in the Washington, D.C., area, you can still find a federal career in your immediate vicinity. For example, if you were interested in the Department of Agriculture, you might find a job in New York City as a USDA market reporter, or you might be on a farm in central Illinois, helping the farmer to combat soil erosion. Each city and state carries its own flotilla of specialists, and it is for you to determine the area of your interest and then head for it. Here are some of the positions your Federal Government can offer the qualified person.

Department of Agriculture

This department is one of the largest and most versatile in the government. Within its confines, it probes deeply into the biological sciences. Agronomy, husbandry, genetics, parasitology, bacteriology, nematology, botany, home economics, mycology, horticulture, plant pathology, plant physiology, plant quarantine inspection, plant pest control, biology, microbiology and entomology are the areas of research. The importance of this department cannot be underestimated. Here much of the pure research so important to the technological advancement of man is initiated. For example, during World War II, previous research on hybridization of grains enabled the government to make recommendations to the farmer that not only increased production, but decreased the number of personnel used on the farms. More men were freed for other vital jobs, and the peoples of the world had more to eat.

Economics—agricultural, international trade, forest, business, transportation, labor and social science analysts; engineering—electrical, telephone, mechanical, chemical, highway, hydraulic, agricultural, architectural, civil, construction, equipment and cartography; agriculture extension; farm management; forestry—foresters, forest pathologists, woodland conservationists and technologists; information—information specialists, editors, motion-picture technicians, artists and illustrators, photographers, and exhibit specialists; inspection and investigation—warehouse examiners, commodity investigators, inspectors, graders and classers; legal—attorneys; library—librarians in most phases of library science; physical sciences—geology, physics, chemistry; soil and range conservation—soil conservation, soil science and range conservation; statistics—actuary and statistics; veterinary science; plus administrative services—are the other departments within the Department of Agriculture.

As of this writing the Department has sixteen operating agencies. Its total full-time employment is about 90,000 people, of which some 80,000 are field employees at 7,500 operations locations; 21,000 employees of the State Extension Services, plus 20,000 attached to State Agricultural Experiment Stations and closely associated with the Department's activities.

One could explore the achievements of the Department of Agriculture for many more pages, but the Department itself has issued some outstanding literature that details its development and opportunities. For more information, write to: Office of Personnel, United States Department of Agriculture, Washington 15, D.C. Be sure to state your specific preference.

United States Civil Service Commission

Specific training other than college or its equivalent is not required. The United States Civil Service Commission has, as one of its functions, the policing of the effectiveness and loyalty of the executive branch of the Federal Government's work force. It is the leader in personnel management within the government. More than two million Federal employees are stationed throughout the United States, its territories and possessions, and in the majority of foreign countries. The need for topflight personnel continues. For further information, write or visit the Director of Personnel, U. S. Civil Service Commission, Washington 25, D.C. (You may also obtain the same information from one of the regional offices listed on page 176).

Job Title	Qualifications	No. of Positions in Government
Accountant	4 yrs. college study incl. 24 semester hours in accounting and auditing	17,000 scattered throughout government
Actuary	4 yrs. college study with courses in math. totaling at least 24 semester hours	50 in Federal services
Administrative Assistant	4 yrs. college study courses in public administration, business administration, industrial management, industrial engineering, political science. Written test.	Numerous and varied
Agricultural Market Reporter	4 yrs. college study in agriculture, economics, marketing, transportation or business administration	More than 600 jobs
Agricultural Marketing Specialist	4 yrs. college study in agriculture, economics, marketing	About 300 jobs
Anthropologist	4 yrs. college study, 20 semester hours in anthropology, incl. one course in Amer. archaeology	About 100 positions
Architect	4 yrs. college study, major in architecture	Wide opportunity, total number undisclosed

Job Title	Qualifications	No. of Positions in Government
Archivist	4 yrs. college study incl. 12 hrs. U. S. history and 18 hrs. history, political science, sociology, economics, or public administration. Written test.	About 350 jobs
Attorney	Membership to Bar	8,000 positions
Biologist	4 yrs. college study, incl. 30 semester hours in biological science.	More than 600 positions
Budget Examiner	4 yrs. college study; for higher grade entrance, graduate work in public administration, business administration, government, political science, economics may qualify	Over 4,700 positions
Business Analyst	4 yrs. college study; for higher grade entrance, graduate work in business administration, business economics, chemistry, physics, etc.	About 500 analysts jobs
Cartographer	4 yrs. college study with major in cartography, geodesy, engineering,	2,700 Urgent need for more trained people

CAREERS WITH THE GOVERNMENT

Job Title	Qualifications	No. of Positions in Government
	mathematics, photogrammetry or physics	
Chemist	4 yrs. college study, incl. 30 semester hours in chemistry	Large group but widely scattered; no figures available
Criminal Investigator	4 yrs. college study, with 18 hrs. in police science, police administration, criminology or law enforcement subjects	About 10,000 positions
Customs Examiner	Federal-Service Entrance Examinations	No figures available
Customs Inspector	Federal-Service Entrance Examinations	No figures available
Dietitian	4 yrs. college study plus 2 yrs. exp. in field	No figures available
Economist	4 yrs. college study, incl. 24 semester hours in economics	About 3,000 Wide choice in many different departments
Education Officer	4 yrs. college study, incl. 18 hours in education	Over 15,000—in almost all govt. agencies
Estate Tax Examiner	Successful completion of course of combined pre-legal and legal study leading to LL.B.	More than 450
Financial Institution Examiner	4 yrs. of college level study in accounting, econom-	No figures available

Job Title	Qualifications	No. of Positions in Government
	ics, banking, finance or business administration	
Food and Drug Inspector	4 yrs. college study incl. 30 semester hours in either or a combination of hours in pharmacy, chemistry, biology, bacteriology, and food technology	No figures available
Geologist	4 yrs. college study incl. 30 semester hours in geology	About 1,500
Historian	4 yrs. college study incl. 24 semester hours in history	No figures available
Home Economist	4 yrs. college study, with major study in home economics or related subjects	No figures available
Hospital Administrator	4 yrs. college study and 1 year of graduate study in hospital administration	No figures available
Industrial Specialist	4 yrs. college study with courses in industrial management or engineering	10,000
Interior Decorator	4 yrs. college study incl. an average of 6 semester hrs. a year in interior decoration or design, architecture, commer-	About 50

CAREERS WITH THE GOVERNMENT

Job Title	Qualifications	No. of Positions in Government
	cial art or related fine arts courses	
Internal Revenue Agent	4 yrs. college study incl. an average of 6 semester hrs. a year in accounting subjects	10,000 (See page 175 for field offices)
Investigator	4 yrs. college study; prefer emphasis on accounting, banking, business administration, economics, etc.	4,000
Landscape Architecture	4 yrs. college study with major in landscape architecture or landscape design	Approximately 300
Loan Examiner	4 yrs. college study, major study in accounting, banking, and credit, economics, finance, law, real estate operations, statistics and business administration	About 1,500
Management Analyst	4 yrs. college study in any major field	About 10,000
Mathematician	4 yrs. college study incl. 24 semester hours in mathematics	No figures available
Medical Record Librarian	4 yrs. college study, incl. 24 semester hours of organic	No figures available

Job Title	Qualifications	No. of Positions in Government
	theoretical courses in a medical record library science curriculum	
Medical Technologist	4 yrs. college study, incl. 6 semester hours in inorganic chemistry and 3 semester hours in either quantitative analysis, organic chemistry, or biochemistry	Comparatively new, but expanding; no figures available
Museum Curator	4 yrs. college study	Somewhat over 50
Nurse	Either full 3-year course in residence or a full 2-year course in residence plus additional experience or education	Numerous and varies; no count available
Personnel Worker	4 yrs. college incl. courses in personnel and public administration, psychology, sociology, political science, business management, economics, statistics, English, and public speaking	12,000
Printing and Publications Officer	4 yrs. college incl. 24 semester hours in accounting, business administration,	800

CAREERS WITH THE GOVERNMENT

Job Title	Qualifications	No. of Positions in Government
	commerce, economics, English composition, printing or printing engineering, industrial engineering, journalism, or graphic or commercial art	
Psychologist	4 yrs. college study incl. 24 hours in psychology with at least one course in statistics. For higher levels, a Ph.D. is required.	No figures available
Purchasing Officer	4 yrs. college study, incl. 24 semester hours in law, business administration, commerce, accounting, purchasing or any other special subject relating to an appropriate commodity	10,000
Quality Control Specialist	4 yrs. college study, incl. 24 semester hours in product management, industrial management, business administration	Several thousand
Realty Officer	4 yrs. college study incl. business administration, finance, law, real estate,	4,000

FROM KITCHEN TO CAREER

Job Title	Qualifications	No. of Positions in Government
	engineering or architecture	
Recreation Specialist	4 yrs. college study with major in recreation, physical education, theater or dramatic arts, music, radio management techniques, speech and drama, vocational and industrial arts, education, art, painting, sculpture or sociology	No figures available
Revenue Officer	4 yrs. college study in any major field	5,000
Social Worker	M.A. in social work	Continuing need; no figures available
Speech Pathologist and Audiologist	All requirements for M.A. completed in either speech pathology or audiology	New but growing field; no figures available
Supply Officer	4 yrs. college study incl. 24 semester hours or equivalent in accounting, business administration or commerce	26,000
Translator	Pass tests requiring a general knowledge of one or more foreign languages	About 500
Writer and Editor	4 yrs. college study, any major	4,000

CAREERS WITH THE GOVERNMENT

INTERNAL REVENUE FIELD OFFICES

Address of Regional Commissioner	*States in Region*
Peachtree-Baker Building 275 Peachtree Street, N.E. Atlanta 3, Ga.	Alabama, Florida, Georgia, Mississippi, North Carolina, South Carolina, Tennessee
55 Tremont St. Boston 8, Mass.	Connecticut, Maine, Massachusetts, New Hampshire, Rhode Island, Vermont
P. O. Box 1144 Chicago 90, Ill.	Illinois, Michigan, Wisconsin
Room 900, Swift Building 230 E. 9th Street Cincinnati 2, Ohio	Indiana, Kentucky, Ohio, Virginia, West Virginia
1114 Commerce Street Dallas 2, Texas	Arkansas, Louisiana, New Mexico, Oklahoma, Texas
90 Church Street New York 7, N. Y.	New York
3407 U. S. Post Office and Courthouse 215 N. 17th Street Omaha 2, Nebraska	Colorado, Iowa, Kansas, Minnesota, Missouri, Nebraska, North Dakota, South Dakota, Wyoming
2 Penn Center Plaza Philadelphia 2, Pa.	Delaware, District of Columbia, Maryland, New Jersey, Pennsylvania
870 Market Street San Francisco 2, Calif.	Alaska, Arizona, California, Hawaii, Idaho, Montana, Nevada, Oregon, Utah, Washington

REGIONAL OFFICES FOR CIVIL SERVICE COMMISSION

Address of Regional Commissioner — *States in Region*

Central Office
The United States Civil Service Commission
Washington 25, D. C.

Atlanta Region—
Federal Bldg.
275 Peachtree St., N.E.
Atlanta 3, Ga.

Alabama, Florida, Georgia, Mississippi, North Carolina, Puerto Rico, South Carolina, Tennessee and Virgin Islands

Boston Region—
Post Office and
Courthouse Bldg.
Boston 9, Mass.

Connecticut, Maine, Massachusetts, New Hampshire, Rhode Island, and Vermont

Chicago Region—
Main Post Office Bldg.
Chicago 7, Ill.

Illinois, Indiana, Kentucky, Michigan, Ohio, and Wisconsin

Dallas Region—
1114 Commerce Street
Dallas 2, Texas

Arkansas, Louisiana, Oklahoma, and Texas

Denver Region—
Building 41
Denver Federal Center
Denver, Colo.

Arizona, Colorado, New Mexico, Utah, and Wyoming

New York Region—
News Building
200 E. 42nd St.
New York 17, N. Y.

New Jersey and New York

Philadelphia Region—
Customhouse
Second and Chestnut Streets
Philadelphia 6, Pa.

Delaware, Maryland, Pennsylvania, Virginia, and West Virginia

CAREERS WITH THE GOVERNMENT

Address of
Regional Commissioner *States in Region*

San Francisco Region— California, Hawaii, and
128 Appraisers Bldg. Nevada
630 Sansome St.
San Francisco 11, Calif.

Seattle Region— Alaska, Idaho, Montana,
302 Federal Office Bldg. Oregon and Washington
First Ave. and Madison St.
Seattle 4, Wash.

St. Louis Region— Iowa, Kansas, Minnesota,
Federal Bldg. Missouri, Nebraska, North
1520 Market St. Dakota, and South Dakota
St. Louis, Mo.

United States Department of Commerce

This is the key agency in the promotion of the nation's business and industry, foreign and domestic commerce, systems of transportation and scientific and technological growth. Some of the activities within the department where the mature woman may be useful are census-taking and surveys of populations, housing, agriculture, industry, business and trade. She might also compile and supply information on domestic and foreign industries and trade, or be a member of a department that publishes technical information developed by and for the Government. Jobs such as the above-mentioned plus others within the department require degrees in such majors as mathematics, cartography, statistics, physics, chemistry, economics, administration, and accountancy. For further information, the following bureaus may be of help: The Bureau of Foreign Commerce, National Bureau of Standards, Office of International Trade Fairs, Office of Business Economics, Business and Defense Services Administration, and Bureau of the Census. Or write to the U. S. Department of Commerce, Washington 25, D.C.

Office of Emergency Planning

As its name indicates, this office is established to provide emergency planning in case of enemy attack. Its work involves emergency government, production, economic stabilization, communications, transportation, manpower and all other areas necessary for the continuation of society's functions. It works closely with all major departments and agencies of the Federal Government. People most acceptable to this department are those who are trained administratively and who also have a good background in the social sciences. Candidates must pass the Management Intern option of the Federal Service Entrance Examination. Appointments are made at both the GS-9 and GS-7 levels. (See page 188 for description of GS levels.) For further information, write to the Director of Personnel, Office of Emergency Planning, Executive Office Building, Washington 25, D.C.

Federal Trade Commission

This commission maintains free competitive enterprise. It is designed to enforce various laws to eliminate unfair, deceptive and monopolistic practices in interstate commerce. Although most of the employment opportunities are for law school graduates, the Commission also has openings for a limited number of college graduates as business economists, accountants, statisticians, investigators, and management assistants. For more information, write to the Director of Personnel, Federal Trade Commission, Washington 25, D.C.

General Services Administration

This is responsible for the management of real property, personal property, archives and records, transportation, public utilities, and procurement and management of the national stockpile for strategic and critical materials. It is the central buying agency for the Government, is worth about ten billion dollars and has about twenty-eight thousand employees. College-trained or college caliber people may find jobs in management, personnel, budget administration, architecture, accounting, archival and records management, procurement, supply, property management and disposal, traffic management, investigation, and law. For more information, write or visit the Director of Personnel, General Services Administration, Washington 25, D.C., or a regional office.

Government Printing Office

This office prints up the Government's garrulity. From the Congressional Record to the material you will receive when you write for more information, the deluge is part of the Agency's ninety-one million dollars' worth of printing. A back-to-work woman might find a job in the employee-relations and personnel categories, in accounting, library work, or in some of the book manufacturing processes, such as proofreading and copy-editing. More information can be obtained from the Assistant Executive Officer and Director of Personnel, United States Government Printing Office, Washington 25, D.C.

Department of Health, Education and Welfare

Some of the widest opportunities to the mature women are probably offered here. It is possible to be a claims representative in one of the five hundred and thirty district offices of the Social Security Administration. Any college degree will qualify for one of these positions. Other social security programs where one can feel productive and useful might be in the departments of maternal care, child health, crippled children and child welfare services; old-age assistance; and aid to the blind, to dependent children, and to the disabled.

If your training is oriented toward the medical, biological and physical sciences, the Public Health Service may be your ideal niche.

For medical school graduates, chemists, bacteriologists, and biological technicians and pharmacologists, the Food and Drug Administration offers excellent opportunity. This is the agency that insures that foods, drugs, therapeutic devices, and cosmetics are pure, safe to use, and truthfully labeled.

The Office of Education collects and disseminates information, has an advisory service, and administers grants-in-aid to education.

The Office of Vocational Rehabilitation cooperates with the States to provide services to preserve, develop, or restore the ability of disabled people to work.

Further information on all of these departments may be obtained by writing to the Director of Personnel for the Department or the personnel office of any of the agencies listed above. Write either to Washington, D.C., or the list of regional offices on page 000.

Housing and Home Finance Agency

This agency has its eye on the physical planning and shelter problems that our expanding population is creating within the urban areas. College graduates with skills in public administration, city and regional planning, finance, accounting, real estate, architecture, law, business administration, political science, and sociology are needed to carry on the functions of this department. For additional information write to the Director of Personnel of any of the following HHFA organizations. All are located in Washington 25, D.C.

The *Community Facilities Administration* loans money for student and faculty housing on college campuses, advances monies for the planning of public works and makes loans to finance construction of public facilities.

The *Urban Renewal Administration* assists in slum blight and reclamation.

The *Federal Housing Administration* loans money for the improvement of residential properties.

The *Public Housing Administration* helps financially in the construction and operation of low-rent public housing for low-income families.

The *Federal National Mortgage Association* helps with home mortgages.

United States Information Agency

Although a relative newcomer in Government agencies (it was established in 1953), the USIA is one of the most fascinating for the liberal-arts-minded. It tells other peoples of the world about the United States. To do this, it uses radio, television, motion pictures, newspapers, books, magazines, pamphlets, and exhibits. It is highly concerned with culture. Although many of its positions are for young people who have no family ties, it does have a limited number of positions such as information clerk, editorial clerk, picture research assistant and news and publications writer. College majors in English, journalism, or international relations are required for these positions. More information can be obtained from the Chief Employment Branch, United States Information Agency, 1776 Pennsylvania Ave., N.W., Washington 25, D.C.

The Department of the Interior

This department watches over natural resources like

a mother hen over her chicks. It husbands the conservation and development of mineral resources and the promotion of mine safety, protection of fish and wildlife, of forest and range lands, the administration of the great scenic and historic areas, and the reclamation of the deserts and arid regions. Its control encompasses not only the continental United States, and U.S. possessions in the Caribbean and the South Pacific, but also the interests of over 400,000 Indians, Eskimos and Aleuts in the United States and Alaska. College graduates may find opportunities in public administration, cartography, physical and analytical chemistry, economics, education, mathematics, physics, social work, statistics, technical editing and writing, and as technical librarians. These opportunities may exist in any of the Department's Bureaus, which are: Bureau of Indian Affairs, Bureau of Land Management, Bureau of Mines, Bureau of Reclamation, Geological Survey, National Park Service, Office of Territories, Bonneville Power Administration, Southeastern Power Administration, Southwestern Power Administration, Bureau of Sport Fisheries and Wildlife and Bureau of Commercial Fisheries. Inquiries may be made to the appropriate bureau personnel office, Department of the Interior, Washington 25, D.C. Special inquiries to the Power Administrations should be made as follows:

>Southeastern Power Administration
>Elberton, Ga.

>Southwestern Power Administration
>P.O. Drawer 1619
>Tulsa 1, Okla.

Bonneville Power Administration
P. O. Box 3537
Portland 8, Oregon

Department of Labor

Jobs are this department's interest—your job and my job. It provides adequate assistance to workers who are looking for jobs and to employers who are in need of workers. It works with the State on employment problems and on the unemployment insurance systems. It supplies labor market information, protects the worker on the job with laws concerning child labor, safety and health standards, wages and hours, workmen's compensation and the rights of union members. College graduates or college caliber people may find interesting positions in administration, auditing and accounting, budgeting, economics, employment security, and unemployment insurance, information and editorial, international affairs, investigation, legal, personnel administration and statistics. The Director of Personnel, United States Department of Labor, Washington 25, D.C., will give further information.

Library of Congress

The Library maintains a vast collection of recorded knowledge. At present, the collection totals more than 36,900,000 pieces! Professionally-trained librarians, particularly those with special fields of knowledge, are in demand, as are college graduates who have majored in social and physical sciences. Foreign language competence is an asset. For more information, write to the Director of Personnel, Library of Congress, Washington 25, D.C.

Post Office Department

About 580,000 employees in some 35,000 post offices are employed by this department throughout the country. Those people who are qualified in accounting and finance, personnel, transportation, organization, and related administrative functions may find positions either with the local post office or in Washington, D.C. Services call for continuous research and examination. More information can be obtained by writing to the Post Office Department, located in Atlanta, Boston, Chicago, Cincinnati, Dallas, Denver, Memphis, Minneapolis, New York, Philadelphia, Seattle, Washington, St. Louis, San Francisco, Washington, D.C., Wichita.

Small Business Administration

In 1953 the Small Business Administration was established for the purpose of assisting the Nation's small business concerns. Its total number of employees is approximately two thousand, but there are sixty field offices in fifty states. College training in money and banking, accounting, business administration, economics and law would fit you for work with the Administration. For further information, contact your local Small Business Administration field office or write to the Director of Personnel, Small Business Administration, 811 Vermont Ave., N.W., Washington 25, D.C.

The Treasury Department

This department superintends and manages the Government's finances plus many other vital fiscal functions. College-trained people in accounting, economics, banking, tax law, business and public administration may find positions in any of the thirteen operating bureaus and offices. These are the Bureau of Accounts, United States Coast Guard, Office of the Comptroller of the Currency, Bureau of Customs, Bureau of Engraving and Printing, Internal Revenue Service, Bureau of the Mint, Bureau of Narcotics, Office of Production and Defense Lending, Bureau of the Public Debt, United States Secret Service, Office of the Treasurer of the United States, and United States Savings Bonds Division. For further information, write to the Director of Personnel, Treasury Department, Washington 25, D.C. For positions in the field, write to the board of U. S. Civil Service examiners at the Internal Revenue office whose jurisdiction covers the State you wish to work in. (See page 175).

Veterans Administration

This is practically a city in itself. It serves our veterans in innumerable ways. About one-third of the positions require professional or college-level training. These positions may include vocational rehabilitation, medical administration, home loans, insurance, compensation and pension, electronic data processing, housekeeping management, supply, budget, finance, personnel and administrative services.

Also special departments have need of accountants, actuaries, counseling psychologists, and lawyers. Various medical technologists such as pharmacists, dietitians, social workers, recreation leaders, physical, corrective and occupational therapists, medical records and general librarians are in great need. And in addition, the biochemists, microbiologists and related specialists in both clinical and research work will find opportunity with the Veterans Administration. Wherever a VA hospital exists, one will also find a full complement of doctors, dentists, and nurses. More information can be obtained at any VA hospital center or regional office and from the Central Office Personnel Service, Veterans Administration, Washington 25, D.C.

In the above description of departments, we have mentioned various job categories for which college training or its equivalent is necessary. College equivalency calls for a background knowledge or satisfactory combination of education and experience in lieu of specific educational requirements. However, if you plan your back-to-work program, you may want to train specifically for any of the following positions listed on the chart. Bear in mind that while these positions do not apply to government alone, in many cases, because of the competitive examinations, the Government may be your best choice.

CLASSIFICATION ACT SALARY RATES

The following tables show pay rates effective in October 1962 and pay rates to be effective in January 1964. Within-grade raises are granted to employees whose work is at an acceptable level of competence at the following intervals: every year for the first three rates, every two years for the next three rates, and every three years for any remaining rates. Within-grade increases may be given more frequently to employees who do high quality work. When an employee is promoted to a higher grade, he must receive a salary increase equalling at least two within-grade increases of the grade from which he is promoted.

THE PAY SCALES OF THE CLASSIFICATION ACT
EFFECTIVE OCTOBER 1962
GENERAL SCHEDULE—BASIC PER ANNUM RATES

Grade	Rate 1	Rate 2	Rate 3	Rate 4	Rate 5	Rate 6	Rate 7	Rate 8	Rate 9	Rate 10	Step Rate
1	$3,245	$3,350	$3,455	$3,560	$3,665	$3,770	$3,875	$3,980	$4,085	$4,190	$105
2	3,560	3,665	3,770	3,875	3,980	4,085	4,190	4,295	4,400	4,505	105
3	3,820	3,925	4,030	4,135	4,240	4,345	4,445	4,580	4,705	4,830	105-125
4	4,110	4,250	4,390	4,530	4,670	4,810	4,950	5,090	5,230	5,370	140
5	4,565	4,725	4,885	5,045	5,205	5,365	5,525	5,685	5,845	6,005	160
6	5,035	5,205	5,375	5,545	5,715	5,885	6,055	6,225	6,395	6,565	170
7	5,540	5,725	5,910	6,095	6,280	6,465	6,650	6,835	7,020	7,205	185
8	6,090	6,295	6,500	6,705	6,910	7,115	7,320	7,525	7,730	7,935	205
9	6,675	6,900	7,125	7,350	7,575	7,800	8,025	8,250	8,475	8,700	225
10	7,290	7,535	7,780	8,025	8,270	8,515	8,760	9,005	9,250	9,495	245
11	8,045	8,310	8,575	8,840	9,105	9,370	9,635	9,900	10,165		265
12	9,475	9,790	10,105	10,420	10,735	11,050	11,365	11,680	11,995		315
13	11,150	11,515	11,880	12,245	12,610	12,975	13,340	13,705	14,070		365
14	12,845	13,270	13,695	14,120	14,545	14,970	15,395	15,820	16,245		425

THE PAY SCALES OF THE CLASSIFICATION ACT
EFFECTIVE JANUARY 1964
GENERAL SCHEDULE—BASIC PER ANNUM RATES

Grade	Rate 1	Rate 2	Rate 3	Rate 4	Rate 5	Rate 6	Rate 7	Rate 8	Rate 9	Rate 10	Step Rate
1	$3,305	$3,410	$3,515	$3,620	$3,725	$3,830	$3,935	$4,040	$4,145	$4,250	$105
2	3,620	3,725	3,830	3,935	4,040	4,145	4,250	4,355	4,460	4,565	105
3	3,880	3,985	4,090	4,195	4,300	4,405	4,525	4,650	4,775	4,900	105-125
4	4,215	4,355	4,495	4,635	4,775	4,915	5,055	5,195	5,335	5,475	140
5	4,690	4,850	5,010	5,170	5,330	5,490	5,650	5,810	5,970	6,130	160
6	5,235	5,410	5,585	5,760	5,935	6,110	6,285	6,460	6,635	6,810	175
7	5,795	5,990	6,185	6,380	6,575	6,770	6,965	7,160	7,355	7,550	195
8	6,390	6,600	6,810	7,020	7,230	7,440	7,650	7,860	8,070	8,280	210
9	7,030	7,260	7,490	7,720	7,950	8,180	8,410	8,640	8,870	9,100	230
10	7,690	7,945	8,200	8,455	8,710	8,965	9,220	9,475	9,730	9,985	255
11	8,410	8,690	8,970	9,250	9,530	9,810	10,090	10,370	10,650		280
12	9,980	10,310	10,640	10,970	11,300	11,630	11,960	12,290	12,620		330
13	11,725	12,110	12,495	12,880	13,265	13,650	14,035	14,420	14,805		385
14	13,615	14,065	14,515	14,965	15,415	15,865	16,315	16,765	17,215		450
15	15,665	16,180	16,695	17,210	17,725	18,240	18,755	19,270			515
16	16,000	16,500	17,000	17,500	18,000						500
17	18,000	18,500	19,000	19,500							500
18	20,000										

Grade											
15	14,565	15,045	15,525	16,005	16,485	16,965	17,445	17,925			480
16	16,000	16,500	17,000	17,500	18,000						500
17	18,000	18,500	19,000	19,500	20,000						500
18	20,000										

A FINAL WORD

You're on your own. The choice is yours. Given a bit of will power, a lot of common sense and real direction, there is no doubt that you will reach the top of your potential. Never say die! All the myths have been exploded: the myth of discrimination against age; the myth that one cannot learn in the mature years; the myth that careers do not exist after forty. Thousands of women are proving otherwise every minute, every hour, every day of the week.

But remember! Getting the job does not mean the end of your achievement. A job can be used as a stepping-stone to a better position, or it can be developed into a better job solely through your own efforts. A job isn't your job until you have made it part of yourself. This holds true for any job, whether it be professional or clerical. Your prospective employer has no way of knowing what he can offer you until you have shown him what you can do.

A case in point occurred right within our own agency. We hired two mature women (over forty) who had never held full-time jobs. They were hired to do simple filing and clerical work. Both of these women became so involved in the agency that they took on more responsibility than we had delegated, but in so doing, relieved the executive staff of some tedious, time-consuming duties. Because they performed so well and with so much integrity, they were promoted within six months—one to the position of collection manager, the other to a part-time placement manager. Now they function independently with equal status to the other professionals in the organization.

We believe implicitly that there is no such thing as a dead-end job. In our fifteen years of experience we have never found a job that could not be filled by the *right* person. Some people kill a job when they are asked to do simple chores such as typing up a statement or running an errand; others willingly accept a job in toto, expanding its limitations with their own life-giving energy. Recently, we placed a young woman as a gal Friday to the publicity director of a large publishing house. After three months on the job, she quit in distress announcing that the job would lead nowhere. We then were asked to fill this job again, but please, our client counseled, be sure that this applicant is realistic about the job's possibilities. This time we sent a woman of similar background, but who impressed us with her desire to perform to the best of her ability, the job at hand. True, she hoped that she would have a chance to use her creative talents, but she did understand that the opportunity might not be readily forthcoming. However, she turned over the apple-cart. After three months of diligent work, she found that she did have time to help out on the more creative aspects of the job. Her imagination and ability were so exceptional that her employer found it better to use her writing talents than her secretarial skills. It was not long before she became a full-fledged assistant. The total time it took her to reach this new status was six months, only three months more than our other discouraged career seeker. And to make a sad story sadder, we find that after a year,

A FINAL WORD

we are still trying to find that "creative" job for our girl #1.

Among the many wise and beautiful thoughts that our late President Kennedy left us, the words: "It is not what your country can do for you, but what you can do for your country" pretty nearly sums up what we have learned about jobs, and as a consequence about life. If we are permitted the license to say: "It is not what the job can do for you, but what you can do for the job," we believe we are stating one of the healthiest attitudes to be assumed in the search for job and life fulfillment.

INDEX

INDEX

"Abstract of Laws Governing the Practice of Osteopathy," 86
Adult education, 45-66
Age
 appearance and, 20-22
 discrimination due to, 4-5
 new careers and, xiii-xviii, 7-8
 statistics on, xvii
 truthfulness about, 24-25
Agencies
 fees of, 10, 27
 professional, 10
American Association of University Women, 62
American Bar Association, 80
American Dental Association, 114
American Dental Hygienist Association, 115
American Home Economics Association, 49, 78
American Hotel and Motel Association, 122
American Institute of Architects, 69-71
American Institute of Interior Designers, 139, 140
American Institute for Property and Liability Underwriters, Inc., 126
American Library Association, 80
American Medical Association, 83
American National Red Cross, 91
American Nurses Association, 119
American Occupational Therapy Association, 84
American Optometric Association, Inc., 85
American Orthoptic Council, The, 87
American Osteopathic Association, 86
American Physical Therapy Association, The, 88
American Psychological Association, Inc., 89, 90
American School, The, 78
American Society of Chartered Life Underwriters, 126
America's Psychologists (Clark), 90
Apicius, 72
Appearance, personal, 5-6, 20-22
Application
 blanks, 28-29
 letter of, 35-36
Architect, Creating Man's Environment (McLaughlin), 71
Architects, 69-71

Barnard College, xv
Belleau, Wilfrid E., 86
Better Business Bureau, 66

197

INDEX

Bonneville Power Administration, 183, 184
Bookkeeping, 108-109
Boston College, 46
Boston University, 46
Boy Scouts of America, 91
Brooklyn College of New York, 46, 53-55
Bureau of Accounts, 186
Bureau of Census, 178
Bureau of Commercial Fisheries, 183
Bureau of Customs, 186
Bureau of Engraving and Printing, 186
Bureau of Foreign Commerce, 178
Bureau of Indian Affairs, 183
Bureau of Land Management, 183
Bureau of Mines, 183
Bureau of the Mint, 186
Bureau of Narcotics, 186
Bureau of the Public Debt, 186
Bureau of Reclamation, 183
Bureau of Sport Fisheries and Wildlife, 183
Bureau of Statistics, xvii
Business, starting a, 144-155
Business and Defense Services Administration, 178

Cabs, driving, 141-142
Cambridge University, 49
Camp Fire Girls, 91-92
Career Blazers, xi, xiv, xv, 3, 5, 14, 16, 23, 24, 26, 56, 95, 97, 107
Career in Osteopathy (Brewster), 86
Careers, professional, 69-92
See also names of careers

Carnegie Corporation of New York, 47, 48 n., 49
Clerical work, 109-110
Clothes, 21-22
Coffman, Mrs. Larem, 125
College(s)
community, 63-64
entrance tests, 40-41
list of, for adult education, 46-47
professional careers requiring, 69-92
See also Education; names of colleges; Schools
Community Facilities Administration, 181-182
Correspondence schools, 64-65, 78, 125
Cosmetology, 131-133
Council on Social Work Education, 91
Court reporter, 104
Cytotechnology, career in, 83

Dental assistants, 113-114
Dental hygienists, 114-116
Department of Agriculture, 164-166
Department of Commerce, 178
Department of Health, Education and Welfare, 180-181
Department of the Interior, 182-184
Department of Labor, 76-77, 184
Dictaphone secretary, 105
Dietetics As A Profession, 74
Dietitians, 71-75
Dietitians in Demand, 74
Direct mail
in job hunting, 10-11
selling by, 158-159

198

INDEX

Directory of Vocational Counseling Services, 41
Discrimination, 4-5
Douglass College, 46, 56

Education, 6, 12, 14-17
  adult, 45-66
  college entrance tests, 40-41
  community colleges, 63-64
  community services schools, 61-62
  correspondence schools, 64-65, 78, 125
  cost of, 65-66
  grants, 83, 84
  home study, 47
  jobs and, 6, 12, 14-17, 45-66, 69-92
  private vocational schools, 62-63
  professional careers and, 69-92
  scholarships, 47-49, 83, 84, 88, 91, 115
  specialized, 57
  state offices of (list), 58-61
  television courses, 65
  See also Colleges; Schools
Education for the Professions, 85
Executive secretary, 105-107

Family, attitude of, 18-20
Fashion, 133-137
Fashion Institute of Technology, 137
Federal Housing Administration, 182
Federal National Mortgage Association, 182
Federal Trade Commission, 179
Fees, agency, 10, 27
Feminine Mystique, The (Friedan), 45
Field of Social Work, The (Fink), 92
Figure aptitude, 38-39
Fink, Arthur E., 92
Florida Institute for Continuing General Studies, 125
Ford Foundation, 53, 55-56
Friedan, Betty, 45
Friedlander, Walter A., 92
Friends, as sources for jobs, 8-9

General Services Administration, 179-180
Geological Survey, 183
Girl Scouts of the U.S.A., 92
Glamour fields, 5, 6-7, 62
Goddard College, 47, 51-53
Government jobs, 7, 8, 163-187
Grants, educational, 83, 84
Guidance Leaflet No. 23, 86

Hair coloring, 20-21
Hartsell, Charles W., 125
Harvard Education Review, 55
Harvard University, 47, 49
Hippocrates, 72
Home Economics, career in, 77-78
Home Economics Careers for You (Phillips), 78
Home Economics as a Profession (Tate), 78
Hostess, 159-160
Hotel occupations, 120-122
Housing and Home Finance Agency, 181-182

INDEX

Institute of Life Insurance, 126
Insurance, selling, 125-127
Insurance Information Institute, 127
Insurance Institute of America, Inc., 126, 127
Intelligence tests, 39-40
Interior decorating, 137-141
Internal Revenue Service, 186
International Correspondence Schools, The, 78
Interview, the, 23-31
  behavior during, 25-31
  do's and don'ts for, 28-31
  fear of, 23
  procedure in, 23-24
  truthfulness in, 24-25
Interviewing, research, 160-162
Introduction to Social Welfare (Friedlander), 92

Jefferson, Thomas, 46
Jews, 5
Jobs
  agency fees for, 10, 27
  business of your own, 144-155
  choosing, 12-17, 98-100
  cosmetology, 131-133
  dentistry, 113-116
  developing technical skills for, 113-143
  education and, 6, 12, 14-17, 45-66, 69-92
  fashion, 133-137
  glamour, 5, 6-7, 62
  government, 7, 8, 163-187
  hospital, 116-120
  hotel, 120-122
  hunting, 3-11
  interior decorating, 137-141
  the interview for, 23-31

Jobs—*cont.*
  letter of application for, 35-36
  office, 93-112
  personal assets for, 5-7, 20-22
  placement managers, 142-143
  professional careers, 69-92
  résumés for, 11, 31-35
  selling, 122-130, 135-136, 156-158
  skills for, 12-13, 37-38, 113-143
  sources for, 8-11
  spare time, 156-162
  taxi drivers, 141-142
  testing for, 37-41
  trainee, 7
Johnson, Lyndon B., xvii
Journal of the American Osteopathic Association, 86

Kennedy, John F., xvii, 193

La Salle Extension University, 78
Law, career in, 80
Legal secretary, 103-104
Leopold, Mrs. Alice K., 77
Letter of application, 35-36
Library Careers (Logodon), 80
Library of Congress, 184
Library science, career in, 78-80
Life Insurance Agency Management Association, 126
Logodon, Irene and Richard, 80

McLaughlin, Robert W., 71
Macy, John W., Jr., 163
Mail order selling, 158-159
Marks, Jason, xii

INDEX

Marston, Mrs. Helen, 56
Mathematical Association of America, The, 81
Mathematics, career in, 80-81
Medical careers, 81-92, 113-120
Medical secretary, 104-105
Michigan State University, 65
Mills, Lawrence W., 86
Modeling, 136
"Modern Franchising," 155

National Association of Cosmetology Schools, Inc., 133
National Association of Insurance Agents, Inc., 127
National Association of Life Underwriters, 126
National Association for Practical Nurse Education and Service, 118
National Association of Real Estate Boards, 124-125
National Association of Social Workers, 91, 92
National Bureau of Standards, 178
National Compendium of Televised Education, 65
National Council of Teachers of Mathematics, 81
National Executive Housekeepers Association, Inc., 122
National Federation of Licensed Practical Nurses, Inc., 118
National Federation of Settlements and Neighborhood Centers, 92
National Hairdressers and Cosmetologists Association, 132-133
National Home Study Council, 64
National Jewish Welfare Board, 92
National League for Nursing, 119
National Manpower Commission, 97
National Park Service, 183
National Retail Merchants Association, 130
National School of Home Study, The, 78
National Science Foundation, 81
National Society of Interior Designers, Inc., 139, 140
Negroes, 4-5
New York State Optometric Association, 85
Newspaper advertisements, 9-10, 35-36
Noble, Robert V., 125
Northeastern University, 47
Nursery care, 47
Nursing, 116-119
Nutritionists, 71-75

Occupational Brief, No. 34, 85
Occupational therapists, 83-84
Office of Business Economics, 178
Office of the Comptroller of the Currency, 186
Office of Emergency Planning, 178-179
Office of International Trade Fairs, 178
Office jobs, 93-112
Office of Production and Defense Lending, 186
Office of Territories, 183
Office of the Treasurer of the United States, 186

INDEX

Opportunities in Osteopathy (Mills), 86
Optometrists, 84-85
Orthoptics, career in, 86-87
Osteopathic Physician and Surgeon (Belleau), 86
Osteopathic Profession, The, 86
Osteopaths, 85-86
Osteopathy as a Career, 86
Overweight, 21

Perlman, Helen Harris, 92
Peterson, Esther, 163
Phillips, Velma, 78
Photography, 7
Physical therapists, 87-88
Placement managers, 142-143
Planning Your Professional Career, Optometry, 85
Portnoy, Dr. Isidore, xii
Post Office Department, 185
Profession of Psychology, The (Webb), 90
Professional careers, 69-92
  See also names of careers
Psychologists, 88-90
Public Housing Administration, 182

Quarterly (Carnegie Corporation of N.Y.), 48 n.
Queens College, 46, 55

Race prejudice, 4-5
Radcliffe College, 47, 49
Radio, course study by, 47
Radio-announcing, 7
Raimy, V. E., 90
Raushenbush, Mrs. Esther, 51
Real estate, selling, 122-125
Real Estate Commissions, 124
Receptionists, 7, 110-112

Registry of Medical Technologists, The, 83
Relatives, as sources for jobs, 8-9
Research interviewing, 160-162
Résumé, the
  preparing a, 31-35
  printed, 11
Roosevelt, Eleanor, 16
Rutgers University, 55-57

Salaries
  architects, 71
  cosmetology, 132
  dental assistants, 114
  dental hygienists, 116
  dietitians, 74
  government jobs, 188-189
  home economists, 78
  hostess, 160
  hotel occupations, 120
  lawyers, 80
  librarians, 79-80
  medical technology, 83
  nurses, 118, 119
  occupational therapists, 84
  optometrists, 85
  orthoptic technician, 87
  physical therapists, 88
  psychologists, 89
  research interviewing, 162
  retail selling, 129-130
  taxi drivers, 142
Sarah Lawrence College, 46, 50-51
Scholarships, 47-49, 83, 84, 88, 91, 115
School(s)
  community services, 61-62
  correspondence, 64-65, 78, 125
  list of, for adult education, 46-47

202

INDEX

School(s)—*cont.*
 private vocational, 62-63
 returning to, 45-66
 tests for college entrance, 40-41
 See also Colleges; Education
Science Research Associates, 85
Scientific/medical careers, 81-92
Secretaries, 95-108
 qualifications, 96-103, 107
 types of, 103-107
Selling, 122-130, 135-136, 156-158
Seven College Vocational Workshops (Barnard College), xv
Shoes, 22
Simmons College, 46
Simplified Business Services, Incorporated, 155
Skills
 developing technical, 113-143
 gaining, 12-13
 tests for, 37-38
Small Business Administration, 146-150, 185
 list of field offices, 151-153
So You Want to Be a Social Worker (Perlman), 92
Social Security Administration, 149
Social Work—An Introduction to the Field (Stroup), 92
Social Work Year Book, 92
Social workers, 15, 90-92
Society for Industrial and Applied Mathematics, The, 81
Southeastern Power Administration, 183
Spare time jobs, 156-162

Special Libraries Association, 80
Stanford-Binet IQ test, 39
State education offices, list of, 58-61
Stenography tests, 38
Stroup, Herbert H., 92

Taxi drivers, 141-142
Teaching, career in, 75-77
Television, course study by, 47, 65
Testing, 37-41
 college entrance, 40-41
 figure aptitude, 38-39
 intelligence, 39-40
 skill, 37-38
 stenography, 38
 typing, 38
 vocational guidance, 41
Therapeutic dietetics, 72-73
Trainee jobs, 7
Training in Clinical Psychology (Raimy), 90
Treasury Department, 185-186
Truthfulness, importance of, 24-25
Tufts University, 46
Typing test, 38

United States Civil Service Commission, 166-177
United States Coast Guard, 186
United States Information Agency, 182
United States Office of Education, 78, 80
United States Office of Information, 81
United States Savings Bonds Division, 186

INDEX

United States Secret Service, 186
University of Chicago, 162
University of Idaho, 125
University of Minnesota, 46, 47-49
University of Oklahoma, 46, 50
University of Rochester, 76
University of Tennessee, 125
Urban Renewal Administration, 182

Veterans Administration, 89, 186-87
Vocational guidance, 41

Webb, W. B., 90
Wellesley College, 46
White, Thurman, 50
Women's Bureau (U.S. Department of Labor), 76-77
Writers, 7

Young Men's Christian Associations of the U.S.A., 90
Young Women's Christian Association, 62, 92
Young Women's Hebrew Association, 62
Your Eyes and Optometry, 85
Your Opportunity as a Lady O.D., 85